IMPROVING
EMPLOYEE PERFORMANCE
through workplace coaching

Earl – In memory of Percis Kilcoy Smith and George Minto Carter, and the gang who exited 42 Todd Street; and to Bernice Carter (nee Pridmore) and Sarah Rachel Carter for their inspiration, support and long lunches over two generations.

Frank – To my wife Pauline, children Penny, Dale and Kirsten, granddaughter Chloe, and my parents Bill and Ella.

IMPROVING EMPLOYEE PERFORMANCE
through workplace coaching

a practical guide to performance management

EARL M A CARTER
FRANK A McMAHON

KOGAN PAGE

London and Sterling, VA

First published in Great Britain and the United States in 2005 by Kogan Page Limited

120 Pentonville Road
London N1 9JN
United Kingdom
www.kogan-page.co.uk

22883 Quicksilver Drive
Sterling VA 20166-2012
USA

© Earl Carter and Frank McMahon, 2005

ISBN 0 7494 4464 9

British Library Cataloguing-in-Publication Data

A CIP record for this book is available from the British Library.

Library of Congress Cataloging-in-Publication Data

Carter, E. M. A. (Earl M. A.)
   Improving employee performance through workplace coaching : a practical guide to performance management / Earl Carter and Frank McMahon.
      p. cm.
   Includes bibliographical references and index.
   ISBN 0-7494-4464-9 (alk. paper)
   1. Employees—Training of. 2. Employee motivation. 3. Mentoring in business.
4. Labor productivity. 5. Performance standards. I. McMahon, F.
A. (Frank A.) ll. Title.
HF5549.5.T7C298526 2005
658.3'14—dc22
                              2005019168

Typeset by Digital Publishing Solutions
Printed and bound in Great Britain by Creative Print and Design (Wales), Ebbw Vale

Contents

About the authors

Earl Carter is Principal Consultant and Managing Director of Workplace Training and Development Australia, National and International Consultancies. His QPDS (Quality People Development System) approach links organization and job needs to continuous employee development, particularly through learning, assessment, coaching and mentoring.

Earl has worked for many organizations in industries such as coal mining, brewing, drilling, pile driving, steel, forestry, superannuation, university, packaging and petrochemical. He has held positions in private enterprise, government and universities.

Frank A McMahon is Principal Consultant, Management Development Australia Pty Ltd. He has implemented people-based performance improvement projects in many organizations ranging from large transnational/multinational companies (including Phillip Morris, Exxon-Mobil, BHP-Billiton, Telstra and Brambles) to significant Australian-based companies in the food, timber, mining and service industries (including Kraft, Forestry Tasmania, AMP, Federal Hotels and Nabalco).

Frank has provided consultancy services for the Australian Department of Social Security (now Centrelink) and worked for both the Victorian and Tasmanian state governments in senior administrative positions in education and continues to provide consultancy services to local government organizations in Australia. He has also held the posts of course designer and visiting lecturer at Monash University (Mt Eliza) and the University of Tasmania.

Introduction

BACKGROUND

We have been talking about people management (or the lack of it) for over 20 years. The key questions we asked were these:

- Why did the management of people never seem to work properly in most of the organizations we had worked in?

- Why were the greater majority of organizations unable or unwilling (or both), to develop standards of performance and/or a code of conduct/ behaviour (let alone maintain them!)?

- Why was senior management not more insistent on day-to-day/hour-to-hour feedback, which seemed to work extraordinarily well for those managers who practised it?

- Why was individual/group development so poorly managed?

It is fair to say that there are thousands of answers to these questions (mostly legitimate) and we could write a very large book attempting to provide all of them and suggestions as to how things might change. Not surprisingly perhaps, some years ago we leapt in a different direction – what was needed we thought, were better training systems – quality training systems.

Supervisors, managers and their co-workers seemed to be attending an awful lot of training courses, but this didn't seem to have the impact on 'on-the-job' performance that it needed to have. In fact many managers were disillusioned with much of the training and development activity going on.

At the time, most training programmes suffered from a lack of measurable, clearly specified outcomes and measured results. Most training programmes were evaluated on the 'Did you enjoy it?' measure, or people sat for a three-hour theory exam. It was rare for any new learning to be assessed on-the-job.

After talking to a large number of senior managers about what they thought of training generally, we got the title for our book – *The Great Training Robbery – A guide to the purchase of quality training*. The book was based on a quality management system framed around international quality standards. The focus of the book is probably more relevant today than it was then – we even spent a good deal of time on the design of performance-based learning and assessment.

Over the next few years it became clear: if better training systems were the answer, what was the question? Obviously we had missed something. This is not to say that lifelong learning and the ability to adapt to an ever-changing environment are not important – on the contrary. It was simply that quality training by itself is not enough and training is only one way individuals learn and are developed.

We started to get close to what we had missed in preparation for Earl's next book, *Return of the Mentor, Strategies for workplace learning*, to which Frank contributed 'From cop to coach – the shop floor supervisor of the 1990s'. This chapter, by its very title, challenged the traditional role of a workplace supervisor, and began to set the ground rules for effective people management. The requirement was for managers to jump outside their traditional cloak and embrace the practice of feedback and coaching as part of their day-to-day activities, both on and off the job.

But the bells rang loudly after we worked together on change management programmes in some major international companies. We were assisting in the reshaping of the organization by moving from where it is now to where it has to be to survive and/or prosper (change management). Most of the line managers (and some senior managers) appeared not to understand people management at all. Where people management was talked about, it was typically in reference to 'after the event' activities (that is, annual performance appraisals) and/or counselling/disciplinary processes – never day-to-day people management issues. There was no emphasis at all on helping their people become successful – no mention of development.

As for annual performance appraisals, few people had a good word to say about them. This validated some research Frank had done in the 1980s, which indicated that even the performance appraisal systems that HR and senior management thought were OK were often treated with disdain by line managers.

We are not the only ones who believe that traditional performance appraisal systems, with their emphasis on an annual review of performance, seldom work. Coens and Jenkins, in an article entitled 'Abolishing performance appraisals'[1] (based on their book of the same name), argue that in the space of 30 minutes, the typical appraisal can 'transform a vibrant, highly committed employee into a demoralized, indifferent wallflower who starts looking for a new job'.

More significantly they reference a survey conducted by the Society of Human Resources Management that found that more than 90 per cent of appraisal systems are not successful. This certainly accords with our experience, but we would ask if _any_ of them can be successful in sustaining excellent performance or improving below-standard performance if they only occur once a year. Coens and Jenkins go on to add that 'hundreds of other studies and surveys' support their conclusions. Some people tell us that perhaps that is the way it used to be with 'old fashioned' so called 'tick and flick' style appraisals, but not our 'new latest model (say) "360° appraisal system" – it works really well,' they say.

When people do say things like this you need to ask what 'works really well' actually means. If it is contended that we actually improve individual and team performance by these 'once a year' activities, we disagree. So too do quite a few other practitioners.

Thackray[2] for instance, in March 2001, seriously questioned the success of performance appraisals (including 360° models). He stated that his conclusions support those of the DeNisi and Kluger study of 131 feedback systems analysed in that study (see page 27).

One of those conclusions was that 'in more than a third of the cases where it was possible to assess the effectiveness of feedback, providing feedback actually hurt subsequent performance'. Clearly such systems are not working as they should and again, to quote Coens and Jenkins, 'performance appraisals impede genuine feedback, and there is no solid evidence that it motivates people or leads to meaningful improvement.'[3]

It is important to recognize that where we are trying to take performance measurement isn't exactly a new idea. Dr Aubrey Daniels, four years ago in an article 'Appraising the performance appraisal'[4] said, 'some experts, in fact, recommend eliminating the performance appraisal altogether. We agree. The people who get them don't like them. The people who give them don't like them. Why should we do something no one likes or thinks is effective?'

Daniels goes on to say that the research on performance appraisals 'has never shown that they improve performance'. More importantly perhaps, Daniels suggests that the best performance appraisal is one that is 'done every day'.

Well we don't *quite* agree with that. What we say is that the line manager should 'intervene' whenever and wherever possible (and necessary) to coach employees. To use Daniels's words, 'if you've got something to say to employees, spit it out, don't wait for annual reviews.' This may be in relation to recognizing excellent performance (or conduct) or to deal with underperformance or poor conduct. The critical issue is that it is dealt with as close to the 'event' as possible. That is what our system is all about. Frequency of formal review (and how extensive that review might be) is dependent upon the circumstances. It could be a 'Well done, keep up the good work', or it may be a review against some predetermined targets. When the formal review does occur it must be one that has no surprises and is balanced in terms of positive feedback. If performance continues to be poor or the conduct unacceptable, then we will move out of the coaching model and implement the necessary counselling or disciplinary procedures to deal with the issue at hand.

Annual reviews are totally inappropriate for raising poor performance or unacceptable conduct – this must be raised with the employee at the time it occurs, and recognition for excellent performance six months afterwards generally loses its punch because it is seen as an after-thought.

Therefore it was amazing to us that here we were in 2005 and most organizations had no system in place to support day-to-day coaching and/or feedback by managers to their people. We suspect it is because many tried, through the annual appraisal approach, but it failed and in frustration they gave up.

Some annual performance appraisals focus on career development, the pay rise, or what conferences people could or should attend, but few concentrate on the day-to-day management of people, their performance or their development.

There is also an issue in some organizations about whose job it is to actually manage the people (and their issues). The approach described in this book places this responsibility with the line managers (supervisors) and team leaders, but in many organizations underperformance and/or other problems are handed to the HR Department to deal with. Whilst HR has a role (to advise), at the end of the day it is the line managers' responsibility to deal with all of the issues their people have, and any performance issues that arise.

Readers will find a good deal of research and writing in the HR management field on performance appraisal and performance management. These are descriptive but often lack the 'how to do it' element that helps achieve its practical application.

We should also say at this point that the approaches to managing and developing employees, expounded in this book, are relevant to all levels of an organization. Anyone who has the responsibility for the performance, behaviour or development of an employee can utilize these approaches. Around the world such people are recognized by many different titles – line manager, supervisor, team leader (or just manager) and a host of industry-specific titles including matron, superintendent, executive chef, principal, director. We use line manager, manager and team leader interchangeably and include in these titles all those people who are responsible in some way for the performance/conduct of another employee.

We talked to some managers about performance appraisal systems as a tool for improving performance. 'My boss doesn't even like doing it', 'It's too complicated', 'A waste of time', are some of the more printable comments made about people management/appraisal processes.

In some organizations we worked in, genuine attempts were made to make the process work but no one was really sure what it was supposed to achieve. In one major organization the main objective was to identify individual/team shortfalls/gaps in competency, and develop plans to overcome them. Sadly these plans fell into a deep, dark hole because managers were too busy to do what needed to be done. The result was people began falling off the edge, losing ground in the constant need to maintain their individual competitive edge. Such behaviour by the organization did little to maintain relationships and over time to attract and retain good people.

Interestingly, the managers who were seen as the real leaders in their organizations agreed that it was the day-to-day, week-to-week feedback about results and the analysis of what went wrong and what went right and why, that actually delivered the results they wanted. These managers believed in developing their people. They didn't talk about it, they did it.

Certainly we had ideas about what might have contributed to the lack of day-to-day people management systems. One such belief was that it is largely a result of the culture of organizations (even industries), or what might be termed the 'mood' of an organization. This is the type of company culture that would encourage the belief that poor performance isn't worth getting concerned about and that it is probably too difficult to do anything about it.

A further contributing factor could also be that the unwillingness of many managers to engage in honest and forthright feedback on performance, often relates to an aversion to conflict – avoidance/suppression of those difficult problems which were associated with poor employee performance, behaviour and/or conflict. Many take the approach of 'Put your head in the sand

and it will all go away' – but of course, usually it doesn't! This is most noticeable in organizations where managers avoid tackling non-compliance in the workplace in a general sense.

One of the things we reflected on was how managers have changed over the period of our lifetime in work. This wasn't just a yearning for 'yesteryear' – it was an attempt to analyse what was different and how this may have affected the approach to managing people.

The best managers we had experienced demonstrated a set of values that led us to respect them. They spent time with us. They genuinely wanted us to be successful. They gave us the opportunity to use our initiative and to learn from our mistakes.

Supervisors and managers today operate in an extraordinarily complex environment. They don't have spare time. The emphasis is on the outputs and the outcomes (as it should be) but often at the expense of the process and the people who operate in the system. There are more rules, regulations, interruptions, distractions and e-mails than there are hours in the day. One example of this is an establishment we know where performance feedback by e-mail is carried out with only one grading – it tells you if you have done anything that is unacceptable.

Time is certainly a problem, but time for feedback has to be built in to the management process. People seek feedback (positive and negative) and development to make them successful in what they do. More than ever, employees want the confidence and competence to be in charge of their careers (and their lives).

Some employees also had great difficulty with the words 'behaviour' and 'conduct'. Clearly they saw any intervention in attempting to forecast how people should behave in their workplace as extensions of behaviourist psychology. Not that many knew the finer points: they saw it as reminiscent of school days – being stood over and having a big stick waved around as a form of control. Moreover, the manager was seen as having the ammunition to 'beat up' people in a subjective way.

Regulations on sexual harassment, bullying, racial discrimination and general community expectations have at least removed these from many workplaces, but poor conduct/behaviour is still there in many others. The approach described in this book ensures that workplace behaviour is on the same plane as workplace performance and is managed accordingly.

The significance of all of these discussions took on a new emphasis during the 1990s. You may recall that this was the decade in which the number of unfair dismissal claims rocketed upwards in all of those countries that embraced the International Labour Organization Charter on employment policies. Employers could no longer hire and fire at will. They needed to have a valid reason, the processes used had to embody what we call the principles of natural justice, *and* the penalty needed to 'fit the crime'. It could not be harsh.

Thousands of cases have been fought in tribunals and courts and while the principles are now clear, every case is different. This book does not attempt to provide you with a fail-safe approach to handling disciplinary matters because there isn't one. What it does do is help you put in place systems and approaches that will, in our experience, minimize the number of dismissals that occur and therefore the risk of a successful unfair dismissal claim. But there can be no guarantees as there is always the exception to the rule and/or the fall-out from human error.

Improving performance management systems

We have written a deliberately tough-minded approach to improving performance management systems in the workplace. Our system will fit any workplace. It builds on years of practical experience which are the credentials of our approach. A total quality management approach (TQM) is implicit in the book. What is not, is the view ascribed to W Edwards Deming, the founder of TQM, that performance appraisal ought to be eliminated. Many TQM proponents claim that performance appraisals were harmful.[5] A competency-based learning (CBL) approach is also promoted... we use it.

Our hope is that effective coaching delivered to the standard we have created keeps most employees well away from the possibility of being sacked for poor performance and/or behaviour. Poor performance and behaviour should be addressed by management long before individuals get to the brink. But, in our experience, this does not happen and people face the sack for the want of good and timely feedback and opportunities to lift their game. When the sack comes, everyone loses. When dismissal is avoided and the behaviour or performance is restored to the standard required, everyone gains!

Our approach emphasizes that, a) sacking for poor performance and behaviour is a bad outcome (but sometimes unavoidable); and b) poor performance/behaviour *can be fixed* so there is no performance and behaviour that makes sacking necessary (or it should happen during the probation period).

The answer is a good performance management system (using our nine principles; see below), that pushes performance and behaviour away from the 'sackable' zone. The key to our performance management approach is coaching and 'real time' feedback (continuous workplace performance improvement), done by individual line managers. Effective coaching practices depend on these line managers.

> Effective coaches = good performance management = few sackings = good workplace relationships and less cost to the organization.

People often associate being sacked with failure. The assertion is that poor performers are sacked and deserved to be.

Our approach to coaching is unique as it demands line managers use both remedial and developmental roles (how you get people up to excellent performance). Under our approach, line managers are not performance supervisors but performance coaches. This is critical for anyone seeking to gain maximum value out of implementing a system that will deliver improved employee performance. Workplace coaching is the vehicle that will deliver results.

Nine principles of a performance management system

The nine principles on which this approach to performance management is based are:

1. Apart from being injured, the worst thing that can happen to anybody in the workplace is to be sacked. (Not far behind is actually doing the sacking!) In many cases where the termination leads to a claim for unfair dismissal, the costs can be horrendous.

2. Most dismissals can be prevented if managers at all levels actively manage their people against performance standards.

3. Excellent people management begins at the time of selection/recruitment and only ends when an individual leaves the organization. The first step is therefore setting expectations at the earliest possible time. It should apply equally to casual and part-time employees.[6] An individual development plan is highly desirable to provide a reference point during the first 6 to 12 months of employment.

4. 'Performance' in the workplace relates *not only* to the person's competence to do the job to the required standard, *but also* includes behaving in a manner that meets the expectations of the organization (which is not just the management!).

5. The cornerstone of 'best practice' people management is regular day-to-day feedback and coaching as close in time to the event as possible (early intervention), supported by formal reviews where there are no surprises.

6. Everyone can be competent in managing people provided they are committed to the concept of early intervention as part of their normal day-to-day activities. Feedback focusing on both the acknowledgement of excellent performance as well as addressing underperformance is another cornerstone of our approach.

7. The use of performance improvement (individual development) plans to deal with the process of agreed changes to the way we do things is essential to give the system some rigour, and ensure people are dealt with professionally in the process (development).

8. These principles apply at every level of the organization and in every organization but need to be purpose built to suit the particular environment.

9. Managing people is first and foremost the responsibility of the line manager. HR is there to assist, guide and coach managers, and ensure that appropriate systems are in place.

Before we get into the detail of the book here are a few comments about the nine points above to help you understand our starting point for the book.

▌ Dismissal comes at a high financial, emotional and personal cost to those involved.

▌ You will never prevent all sackings, but you can certainly reduce the number if people are actively managed.

▌ Managing people begins with the establishment of standards of performance and codes of behaviour (conduct) which clearly state the organization's expectations in respect to a particular job and the workplace generally. Potential employees need to be advised of the standards of performance and conduct expected _before_ they accept the position. If we were better at communicating expectations during the selection process we might not employ so many people who do not 'fit' with the organization.

▌ As you would have gleaned from the paragraph above, we will not shy away from talking about _conduct/behaviour_ in the same sentence that we talk about _competence_ – they are inseparable. It doesn't matter how skilled someone is, or knowledgeable or compliant with performance standards they are in their job (competent). If they are disruptive to the work team (in terms of bullying, lack of cooperation, sexism, or a 'couldn't care less' attitude towards safety), who wants them? (In the employees' defence, how much effort have we as managers put in to communicating to employees what is expected of them in terms of conduct/behaviour _before_ someone actually does something 'unacceptable'?)

Best practice in managing people relates to early intervention and an effort to correct underperformance, or recognize excellent performance at the first available opportunity.

Managers must actively coach their people if they are to improve. With commitment to engage in regular coaching *plus* some skills training, any-one can be an effective coach. Providing the coaching system itself is built on solid foundations (which we talk about later), the more often you practise and consolidate what you have learnt, the more competent and confident you become (and so does the team). In short, coaching to us represents conscious behaviour towards another person designed to en-courage and support them and make them more successful in their chosen career. It may be confined to specific planned coaching sessions or deliv-ered intermittently in the form of unplanned interventions to provide feedback or impart skills, knowledge and change behaviour.

Performance improvement (individual development) plans simply set down agreement between line managers and their people as to what they will do to bring about agreed changes and/or achieve an agreed level of results/outcomes. A critical aspect of this is the 'learning' that the person and his or her coach agree has to occur and how that is to be achieved. Far too much emphasis is placed on formal training over and above other activities to bring about performance improvement. Training is only one method by which a person can learn, be developed and improve, and valuable as it often is, it is not the only way. There are many other activities such as mentoring or coaching, job rotations, secondments, project work, work improvement programmes or a new job placement (to name a few). The emphasis should always be on selecting the best course of action to achieve the standard of performance and/or behaviour required.

At the upper levels of the organization, performance improvement plans identify and document:

- key result areas;
- performance objectives;
- key performance indicators;

and describe the activities/projects/actions to be undertaken during the life of the plan with review dates, milestones, end dates and person(s) responsible for the activity. More on the upper levels later. At the lower end of the organization, the plans relate to particular aspects of job perfor-mance and may involve further development of capability through formal learning or other developmental strategies (including those that establish and maintain high standards of conduct/behaviour in the workplace).

In this book we draw examples from all of the places we have worked. Whether it be a sugar mill, a timber mill, a government department, a hotel, a meat works, a coal mine, a sporting team, a school or a university – people want to know what is expected of them. Even family members need to clarify expectations of each other to live in harmony. People want to be engaged in communication; they want feedback; they want to get better and enjoy their work; they want some security *and they want to be developed*. If they don't fit, they want to know early on so that they can do something about it. Only someone who is truly desperate wants to hear those words – 'You're sacked!'

ABOUT THIS BOOK

The key to the structure of this book, we believe, is *simplicity*.

Chapter 1. This approach to managing people relies on workplace coaching. Included is an overview and explanation of the key activities that drive this approach to people management. The emphasis is on the development of approaches that are easy to comprehend, learn, put into practice (do), and maintain.

Chapter 2. This deals with how you can get started in the development and implementation of workplace coaching, in particular the processes associated with the development of performance standards and code of conduct based on work expectations. Working examples of these expectations and suggestions for dealing with a workplace out of control are provided. To support this we provide two case studies as Appendices 2 and 3 – one from a production industry, the second from a service industry.

Chapter 3. The focus of this chapter is how to set the scene for workplace coaching by examining how important it is for each manager to be involved in getting the right people on their team through performance-based selection and induction. We make it clear that workplace coaching is the cornerstone of this approach to people management and describe the features of a coach, the activities involved, the principles that support the activities, and how and where these activities are applied in the workplace.

Chapter 4. How a manager operates on the job, day-to-day amongst the team whilst they work, is discussed here. The importance of the quality and integrity of evidence in relation to managing people to achieve excellent performance is stressed. A tool for giving feedback is provided and techniques for acknowledging excellent performance and targeting improvement/development for underperformance discussed.

Chapter 5. This chapter is about how a manager needs to operate off the job through the conduct of a formal review with each member of the team. The importance of the context within which this review must operate, followed by a structured approach on how to do it, is given. The structured approach provides clear guidelines for designing a formal review, including how to develop indicators of performance, and develop and mark rating scales.

Chapter 6. How can managers prepare so that they are able to coach competently and confidently in the workplace? The chapter provides a building-block approach to managing the learning process involved. The building blocks deal with making learning right, making it work, making it connect, making it stick, and checking learning is successful. Also included are guidelines and examples for the learning activities that should be used to develop competence and confidence. It provides an overview of the key features of learning design to develop coaches so that they can implement the actions described in Chapters 1 to 5.

Chapter 7. This chapter looks at how to respond when reality strikes: when it becomes clear that a person is not going to improve his or her performance or behaviour no matter how hard the manager tries to help. All of a sudden someone is likely to be sacked. Clear guidelines are provided as to the process that should be followed, in particular the procedures and rules which govern the management of poor performers.

Chapter 8. This chapter discusses how you might forecast the impact of managing people in your workplace. The importance of developing expectations and consideration of associated costs of doing so as the 'insurance cost' are considered. If your organization has a serious underperformance problem or a major breach of conduct standards, using these approaches can save you money in the long run.

Chapter 9. The difference between seizing the day as opposed to holding your breath until the culture within the organization is reshaped, and what needs to be done, is made clear. The case is argued that the best way to improve the management of your people is to just do it. A starting point is provided along with what needs to be done and how.

Throughout the book we use a range of terminology to describe various approaches and management concepts. So there is no misunderstanding about what we mean, we have included in Appendix 1 a number of these terms and our definitions. You may wish to read this appendix in advance or use it as needed for reference purposes.

ACKNOWLEDGEMENTS

We must thank those people who read the book ahead of its publication, for their assistance and input. Any errors or omissions, of course, are ours. In particular we thank those colleagues and friends who read the earliest versions of the book: Karen Field, Ian Gribble, John Mortensen, Gerry

Rickard, Glen Fawcett, Alan Johnstone – a group of people with senior management experience in the mining, food, hospitality, sugar, education and finance industries. We also thank our wives Bernice (Carter) and Pauline (McMahon) for their input, suggestions and support.

NOTES

1. Coens, T and Jenkins, M (2001) 'Abolishing performance appraisals', _Innovative Leader,_ **10,** 7, 1

2. Thackray, J (2001) 'Feedback for real', _Gallup Management Journal,_ March

3. Coens, T and Jenkins, M (2001) 'Abolishing performance appraisals', _Innovative Leader,_ **10,** 7, 1

4. Daniels, A (2001) 'Appraising the performance appraisal', _Entrepreneur.com,_ July 1–2

5. _Performance Appraisal,_ Wilf Ratsburg, www.geocities.com/athens/forum/3126/htmlperfapp.html2005153

6. Similar principles can be applied to contract management for contractors' work, but beware of the control test – don't apply this system to the contractor's employees.

1

Managing people

Most traditional people management systems have typically concentrated only on an annual review – the lead up to the annual review and the setting of objectives/results for the coming 12 months. These events have a place in the overall system of managing the performance of our people, but this approach treats such snapshots (if they occur at all) as a 'by-product'.

WHO IS THE APPROACH FOR?

This system is designed to be most useful at the middle management and operational levels, especially to all the line managers within the organization. It is also for all the people (work team) who work with these managers. Employees need to know what is expected of them and how their future development will occur. The key points in this approach are:

- clearly defined expectations (at selection, recruitment and induction);

- the manager operating as a workplace coach;

- the manager providing feedback as close to any event as possible (early intervention); this must also be a two-way process;

- no surprises to an employee receiving formal feedback (off the job);

- having a common language of standards of performance and code of conduct (workplace behaviour) that individuals and groups identify with as much as managers;

- feedback should be seen as an ordinary event in a working day – just as a player is given feedback throughout a game, or an actor is given feedback by the director during the filming of a scene;

- genuine two-way feedback between the giver and receiver, which encourages improved workplace outcomes/results;

- the continuous development of each employee in line with expectations, which are continuously renewed in line with the way performance has to change and be improved.

KEY FEATURES

Two of the main features of this approach are that the performance management system must be, a) purpose-built, and b) simple. A purpose-built approach for each organization is important in ensuring that both managers and employees feel a sense of ownership in the system – this is critical to its success. The approach must be brought to life by the involvement of all. This is a dynamic process so the 'building' must be ongoing and reviewed over time. Furthermore, the approach must also be easy to comprehend, learn and put into practice (do) and maintain. Without simplicity, implementation cannot be pursued and sustainable success is put at risk.

Figure 1.1 identifies the key features, aspects and activities of this approach. What is important is to focus immediately on the functions of:

- managing;

- people;

- performance;

- development.

These represent the drivers of this approach, and the activities which support each of these ensure it works.

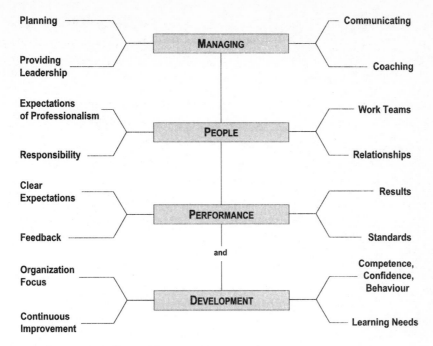

Figure 1.1 A people management approach

Managing

There are a multitude of textbooks that describe what management is all about. In simple terms, we see it as getting things done through people and the available technology. What is required of the line manager in terms of competence is not a subject for this book, other than to identify those functions that must be carried out competently if people performance is to be managed effectively.

This function is critical as the others will succeed or fail depending on how well this approach is managed by:

▌ planning the people management approach with other managers and team members;

▌ providing leadership through commitment and role modelling;

▌ communicating the people management system to all those affected by it;

▌ coaching the work team.

It goes almost without saying: projects as complex as introducing a new people management system require careful planning. We use standard project planning techniques to set up the project plan for the introduction of our people management approach based on workplace coaching.[1] The plan will usually identify:

▪ the project team (leader/sponsor and other team members);

▪ clear objectives;

▪ outcomes/outputs;

▪ methodology;

▪ risk analysis and prevention/mitigation plans;

▪ timeframe/milestones;

▪ cost/benefit;

▪ evaluation strategy.

We recommend this formal approach to project planning and management as important risk prevention/mitigation strategies in themselves – it ensures all of the key players have 'signed off' on the process before it is launched.

There is much debate about what leadership is and we don't propose to add to it. However, it is worth noting that effective people management is an essential aspect of strong leadership. Workplace coaching is the vehicle for exercising leadership and success will be determined by the level of commitment to the expectations (agreed or determined) and the demonstration of professionalism by the line managers (and their teams). To take an organization down this pathway and to succeed requires strong leadership and role modelling by all line managers – they must accept accountability for performance in their workplace and lead their team members through the processes to put a quality people management system in place.

The communication should not be about consulting and convincing managers and team members that people management is necessary. It is about ensuring that they become committed to this particular approach (using workplace coaching with predetermined performance standards and a code of conduct to drive excellent performance). To achieve this, the organization will need to ensure that it provides the necessary resources and training.

Chapter 3 deals with coaching in considerable detail. In essence, we use the word to describe a set of interrelated activities:

- clarifying expectations in regard to results/processes and behaviour;

- providing feedback in the workplace as close to specific work events as possible (early intervention), being always vigilant for timely opportunities to give feedback;

- developing plans to improve individual or team performance and/or to recognize excellent performance (including follow-up).

People

This aspect of our approach deals with:

- The members who make up the work team(s) in the workplace. It is their job to accept responsibility for, and succeed in achieving, the required results.

- In return they have the right to expect professionalism from the manager, coach or director who is managing their performance and development.

- People should know clearly what is expected of them and deserve to be treated with honesty, respect and dignity. People should also expect mental toughness from their manager, who operates by the courage of his or her conviction whilst upholding the principles of natural justice. These are the foundations for successful workplace teams.

These points are critical in the development of harmonious workplace relationships which encourage people to work together in a safe and enjoyable manner.

Performance

Simply put, this means achieving the required results. Whilst many organizations try to come to grips with 'people management' (as in the number of products/services produced in a given time to a given standard) there is an absence of providing coaching and good feedback processes about individual and group conduct/behaviour.

The key element of this approach is that the two (outputs and behaviour) go hand in hand. The driving force behind success is the establishment of clear expectations about:

- the tasks that are to be performed;

- how they are to be performed (process/system);

▌ the standard of the outputs (results);

▌ the behaviour/conduct required in the workplace.

Performance is driven by:

▌ clear expectations of individual employees;

▌ the competence and confidence of employees to perform their work;

▌ a happy and safe work environment (quality work relations);

▌ job satisfaction;

▌ the recognition and rewards given.

Clearly then, conduct/behaviour cannot be left out or treated separately. Remember, this is not just about the elimination of bad/illegal behaviours (for example, bullying, harassment, discrimination) but about the building of good and worthwhile behaviours (respect, helping out, sharing and support for other team members). The code of conduct and coaching can guide people to support and deliver this.

Development

Key result areas are determined at the strategic level of the organization. They are then translated into strategic objectives and flow down into a set of actions to be undertaken. These actions ultimately affect the performance required of people on the shop floor/workplace.

It has been our experience that most managers are not conscious of how changes in key result areas directly impact on the performance of their people. Scant attention is too often paid to the importance of individual/team development plans to deal with agreed changes and subsequent changes in expectations. This moving of the goal posts is very frustrating to people and confuses them – expectations are no longer clear. The individual/team development plan should be seen as a never-ending, continuous improvement process.

Whilst individuals have the right to pursue their own development, it is an imperative to negotiate tight connections between the focus and needs of the organization and the needs of the individual and team. In maintaining the competitive edge of each person, the competitive edge of the organization is also developed.

There is often too much emphasis placed on training needs rather than learning needs when focusing on development. Training is only one way of learning – there are other ways and these need to be considered in line with the nature of the performance improvement required. These may include:

- mentoring;
- work shadowing (spending time with a top performer);
- job rotation;
- exchanges;
- projects.

Success in continuous improvement has a better chance when all managers and their people see lifelong learning as a necessity and ultimately the way of the future.

A PURPOSE-BUILT APPROACH

This approach incorporates the functions and activities of the management team to make sure that the expectations and standards are understood and complied with across the entire work team.

It is about the design, roll-out/implementation of the people management approach in ways that ensure it becomes an integral part of the way the manager and the team think and act as they go about their daily work activities.

It is as much about developing confidence in the coaching system and an acceptance of coaching in the workplace from a conduct/behaviour point of view as it is about the actual products/services produced.

People want to enjoy their work, be excellent at what they do, and most look for recognition of their performance as a major determinant in the level of job satisfaction that they can achieve. Above all else, people want to be developed.

Simplicity of the approach

Simplicity is the key: simple, straightforward and natural in that it becomes part of the everyday life and existence of the individual and teams. Just like serving a customer, making a product, or taking a break – it is part of 'what we do around here' every day. Good performance management becomes a habit of successful workplaces.

This approach thrives as part of everyday organizational life when there is confidence that it is:

* fair;

* consistent;

* honest;

* developed with the involvement of employees.

Giving and/or receiving positive or negative feedback should not be seen by team members as anything special or extraordinary: it is simply part of the way the organization 'does business'. It is not exceptional but part of modern work practices. The extent to which it is *positive and constructive*, and followed up by activities to address underperformance or recognize excellent performance, will determine the way feedback is perceived in the workplace.

The objective of this approach is to remove any threat or discomfort people may feel in giving or receiving feedback. Team members have a right to expect management to be committed to give this feedback in ways that are respectful to them as people, and where the feedback is dealing with underperformance then the line manager will work with team members to achieve the necessary improvement. This will need a total commitment to continuous employee development. It never ends.

In summary, this approach concentrates on the workplace events as they occur, with feedback and coaching to be provided continuously and as close to the event as possible. While there is nothing wrong with monthly, quarterly or annual reviews, they are after-the-event, historical 'by-products' of the people management system. They are not the main game. The main game is the provision of feedback and coaching to team members on a day-to-day basis as part of a normal management role.

It also works to ensure there are no surprises at some point down the track (like a monthly review) which can be very frustrating for team members. There is nothing worse than being told long after the event that your performance or behaviour was unsatisfactory.

This chapter concludes with a *caution*. The upfront requirement of management to be totally committed to the principles and practice of a people management approach is mandatory. Almost every unsuccessful people management system can be traced to inexperienced, poorly trained and uncommitted management, and a lack of good business leadership.

The approaches included in this book should be part of everyday management:

- clear expectations (both ways);

- early intervention;

- recognition of excellent performance;

- a plan to eliminate poor performance.

We now turn to Chapter 2, getting you started in the development and implementation of workplace coaching, in particular the processes associated with performance standards and a code of conduct based on work expectations.

NOTE

1. As consultants we become the planners, along with selected managers and employees. We apply our coaching strategy to ensure the knowledge, tools and skills are retained in the organization.

2

Getting started

We start this chapter by asking six questions:

1. Do you have workplace performance standards and a code of conduct in place and operating at your workplace?

2. Do you know what these standards and code are?

3. Do people comply with them?

4. Do the team members themselves advise their teammates about any underperformance?

5. If you don't have either performance standards or a code of conduct, do you know how to go about developing them, and what is required for them to be accepted and practised in your workplace?

6. Are managers in your organization strictly focused on the product/service? Do they only see the 'people' factor as deserving attention when something goes wrong?

It matters little at this stage how you answered any of these questions, because they are simply aimed at getting you thinking about the current state of your workplace. This chapter will allow you to review your current workplace practices and, where necessary, adjust your current approach. What we would say, however, is that unless you are prepared to go to the effort of documenting performance standards (or at least the critical ones), and a code of conduct with input from those people who will live with them, the system we propose can't work.

ESTABLISHING CLEAR EXPECTATIONS

We see expectations as the driving force in establishing the minimum acceptable performance standards for the key result areas of your particular organization. What is essential to the success of people management systems is that there is a clear, visible link between the strategic objectives of the organization and the expectations of performance we have of everyone in the organization. Key result areas are not selected at the work team level: they are derived from the strategic objectives and flow down.

If an organization is, for example, pursuing strategic objectives related to market growth, this will be reflected in the key result areas of the senior managers. In turn, the specific managers responsible for market growth will also have this key result area broken down into a set of actions to be undertaken so that the market growth objectives can be achieved.

These will be accompanied by appropriate key performance indicators (which allow the success of the actions to be measured on a timely basis). The next linkage is the most critical and the most often overlooked: for all of those people whose performance impacts on the success or failure of the market growth strategy, their performance should be linked to the process through the development of performance criteria against which they can be measured.

Key result areas will almost always include customer service, quality, occupational health and safety, plus areas of performance specific to the organization. Levels of sales (retail), security (banks), hygiene (food or health) and environment (manufacturing/processing) are some examples of those key result areas on which people will have a considerable impact and which will need to be incorporated into the system. Some examples of performance standards are listed further on in this chapter.

These additional key result areas have not always been seen traditionally as worthy or necessary of measurement and control in an organization. We observe that there is a much greater interest now in broader aspects of performance through the 'Balanced Score Card' approach, or similar, with many different aspects of performance now being measured rather than just profitability.[1]

However, we believe that an organization in the 21st century will not perform at the optimal level (and sustain that performance) without also dealing effectively with workplace conduct/behaviour. This is not simply about minimizing unfair dismissals or protecting the organization against harassment or bullying claims – it goes much further. It is about providing a happy and harassment-free workplace. It is about providing an environment where the 'them and us' mentality is eliminated (or at least diminished) because all levels of the organization are committed to the same set of rules – a code of conduct which sets the standard for conduct/behaviour within groups and between groups.

The conduct/behaviour we seek is about delivering real teamwork – where people genuinely look after each other's interests and accept that all of us have both rights and obligations. It is about determining these rights and obligations and complying with them because they work, rather than being driven by a cloud of threats. It is about professionalism in the art of managing people – respect, dignity and principles of natural justice.

Evidence that a coaching-based approach provides a solution comes from a variety of sources. Our own experience, from a range of organizations and companies with which we have worked, is that clarity of expectations, early intervention and regular feedback (both positive and negative) remove uncertainty and have provided significant improvements in workplace behaviour for many organizations.

Our anecdotal evidence is also supported by others. Writing in the _Gallup Management Journal_, [2] John Thackray quoted Professors Angelo S DeNisi and Graham N Kluger in the February 2000 issue of the _Academy of Management Executive_: 'the positive effect of feedback on performance has become one of the most widely accepted principles in psychology'.

Thackray's article, 'Feedback for real' states that 'a series of simple workplace questions can spark employee-management action with measurable results. The effects are local and team-based but they can be repeated across the entire company for bottom-line gains'. 'Feedback for real' pursues the Gallup organization's desire 'to create a better feedback process'.

The feedback process is based on 12 questions posed in surveys (worker interviews) in a range of organizations. These questions translate into key employee expectations that ultimately form the foundation of strong feelings of engagement. Thackray goes on to note 'the process yields actionable input from staff and managers for changes in attitude, conduct, policies and processes'. The tool developed by Gallup has repeatedly been used in 87,000 divisions or work units with 1.5 million employees.

Of the 12 questions posed by Gallup in the survey, 10 are key foci in our book. We have modified them into familiar language, but acclaim their importance in managing people through clear expectations and regular feedback.

THE 10 KEY QUESTIONS

1. What is expected of me at work?

2. Do I have the opportunity to do what I do best each day?

3. Have I received recognition or praise for good work in the last seven days?

4. Does someone at work care about me as a person?

5. Is someone encouraging my development?

6. In the last six months, has someone at work talked with me about my progress?

7. Do my opinions count?

8. Does the mission statement of my company make me feel my job is important?

9. Are my fellow employees committed to doing quality work?

10. In the last year, have I had opportunities to learn and grow at work?

How do we do this?

First, you need to decide if you want to do it. You then need to plan the best way of getting your people 'on board' and be sufficiently supportive to go through the ongoing exercise of developing these expectations and committing to them.

How much consultation?

As much as your organization can sensibly afford in financial and risk management terms.

In relatively 'closed' institutional organizations or work groups, the answer is not much. For example, it is unlikely we will consult with prisoners about our expectations of them (but it might work!) The emergency services have a dilemma here because when they are 'on active service' it is typically in command mode and little consultation can or will occur. When they are not fighting fires, rescuing people or arresting suspects, however, they, like most people, would like that happy, safe and supportive workplace we spoke of earlier. In this domain, a code of conduct is becoming commonplace because such organizations would be dysfunctional without them.

Our experience has been that organizations/industries have been particularly slow or unwilling to pursue a code of conduct and make people comply with them. As discussed earlier, much of this has been related to conflict avoidance.

In a factory, shop, university, school, office or coal mine, the only limitation to the amount of consultation is time (because time is money). However, the process requires:

1. A communication plan, to enlist support from both line managers and team members.

2. Setting up a small representative steering group or groups.

3. Development of draft standards and a draft code of conduct, or codes, for example enterprise-wide and group-specific.

4. Circulation to all affected persons of the draft documents and discussion/refinement.

5. Completion of performance standards/code of conduct.

6. Training of all those affected with a clear understanding of how management and team members should deal with non-compliance.

7. Development of line managers as workplace coaches.

8. Implementation of workplace coaching throughout the organization.

There will also be a need for ongoing evaluation and review from the moment the system is put in place. This will involve providing feedback to the coaches themselves.

Whilst the approach described above is simple and straightforward, in practice there will inevitably be some problems in the successful (and timely) delivery of these steps. If the organization is relatively small, it is usually quite easy to work through the eight steps. As you might imagine, a small workshop or retail establishment should not have too much difficulty in completing the process fairly quickly and without any major upsets. With larger and more complex organizations, whilst this approach is designed to be simple, our experience suggests each step requires considerable thought before implementation. (We suggest a formal project management approach for larger organizations.)

1. Communicating the approach

Senior management need to sit down and design a communication plan. Some companies have referred to this as a 'marketing plan', but this could send the wrong message. While there is some 'selling' required in the communication, we would defy anyone, having heard how the workplace coaching is to operate and what it is designed to achieve, to say, 'We don't need it'! Nonetheless, a careful explanation is required of what we want to do and why, and to allow some two-way feedback about how it might best work for the particular organization. (This is often more successful where it is facilitated by an outside person who is free of 'baggage' from within the organization.)

2. Setting up the consultative process

This step is simply deciding how many groups of what size we need to develop the standards and codes (expectations). The real risk here is people going overboard, either in wanting to have so many performance standards as to frighten everyone off or to have them written in an absurd amount of detail. This has to be managed very carefully as it has been known to bring a system down before it begins – it is all about balance. We still have to run a business!

3. Development of drafts

The developmental processes are discussed in more detail later on in this chapter.

4. Circulation

The circulation of the drafts and the revision of the draft standards again have to be carefully managed. At the end of the day, we are seeking agreed standards – but not agreement at the cost of lowering standards to a level unacceptable to management. If in doubt, trial them. If they are not achieving the results required, amend them. They should never be set in stone, but once they are working they should not be changed too often – again, it is about balance. Managers of organizations who are required to operate under a safety case regime, for example in hazardous industries, will tell you that standards need to be living – they need to change according to the circumstances where necessary.

5. Completion

As stated, they will never be final, but they do need to be signed off by the relevant people in the organization prior to setting up training.

6. Training

One of the most common mistakes made by organizations that are introducing people management systems, is to train the providers of the feedback/coaching – but not the receivers. In this approach, that training starts with the communication plan, continues through the developmental period and culminates in formal training for all participants.

7. Development of line managers as workplace coaches

This is the subject matter of the next chapter.

8. Implementation

This is what Chapters 3, 4, 5 and 6 are about – making it happen, monitoring and review, and continuous improvement in the standard of workplace coaching, as well as overall performance and conduct.

What if the workplace is out of control?

While consultation with strong input and involvement from employees is the preferred way forward to introduce workplace coaching, we have encountered situations where the consultative approach is not going to work in the short term. By 'out of control' we mean:

- people ignore most of the rules (safety, dress, housekeeping);

- absenteeism is high;

- bullying/sexual harassment is a regular occurrence;

- the quality of work is poor;

- good communication is lacking;

- there are high levels of conflict (management-team member; team member-team member; manager-manager);

- there is a lack of interest in problem solving or continuous improvement.

Under these circumstances, the expectations may have to be imposed. From a risk management position you have no alternative, and you might be surprised at the level of support you get from your better employees – few people actually want to work in a poor environment.

Whilst we would say that there should still be some consultation, it would be in response to the management-designed performance standards and code of conduct. Risk management principles don't allow the organization the luxury of lengthy consultation in circumstances of extremely poor performance. We have an obligation to treat the risk as soon as it is identified. Remember, a serious breach of workplace standards (or legislation) could seriously damage the organization.

We have been involved in introducing people management systems in large companies which had to face this problem and bitter employee resistance to any performance feedback system at all. While the imposition of standards of performance and code of conduct was not the ideal way of doing things – it did produce the results required in most instances. (See the case study in Appendix 2.)

THE DEVELOPMENT PROCESS – CODE OF CONDUCT

In terms of the code of conduct, we would expect that it would usually be expressed as 'dos or don'ts', or as a commitment to behave in a certain way. You can set them out any way you wish so long as you test or pilot them to ensure that everyone understands what they mean in practice.

If we are going to say that we will not use inappropriate language in the workplace, people need to understand what that means. Do we mean:

I no swearing in the workplace;

I some swearing in the workplace;

I swear as much as you like but not at any other team member;

I swear as much as you like until someone tells you they think it's inappropriate?

Obviously the answer lies in the individual workplace. At the end of the exercise, all aspects of conduct that are likely to unsettle the workplace or offend individual team members should have been worked through and agreement reached.

It needs to be made clear that management in the end must accept or reject the standards. Team members need to understand this. We have often worked with managers before the development process begins to ensure that they, as a group, have an agreement about what needs to be included.

We would suggest you do not, however, table the manager's views in the discussions, but rather use it as a checklist to make sure nothing has been missed. If the employees can come up with the code by themselves, all the better. Our experience is that the employees will come up with the bulk of the matters to be included and management will just need to fine tune the content.

In some businesses the code may include requirements on dress and general appearance. If this is a change from what people were told when they were appointed, be careful! Changes to conditions of employment cannot simply be imposed – they need to be agreed. In such instances a negotiated outcome will be required.

Some examples of the areas to be included and matters that would generally be addressed in a code of conduct are:

- time management (punctuality, return from breaks);
- attendance (time off, notice, communication);
- team relationships (respectful towards each other, language);
- procedure for leaving the work station/work area.

You will of course include whatever you believe needs to be included. There may be some issues with smoking, inter-racial relationships, or whatever else impacts on delivering a happy, safe and productive workplace.

To conclude, we have listed some extracts from a code of conduct, developed and supported by both managers and employees, on how they will work with each other and treat customers.

EXTRACTS FROM A CODE OF CONDUCT

- Be at (or return to) our workplace meeting/training venue ready to commence at the agreed time.
- Notify any absence to the appropriate person as early as possible.
- Respond to all customers and all employees with respect and in a friendly and timely manner.
- Respect the value and contribution of every employee regardless of what they do.
- Respect the privacy/confidentiality of all customers/employees – mind your own business.

In other codes of conduct we see such things as 'zero tolerance on touching, manhandling and horseplay', or 'helping out your colleague when they need you'. In the end, it has to be developed with the employees in the workplace to reflect that workplace's needs and preferably in a way that will give ownership to the employees. The establishment of clear expectations in these behaviours is essential to minimize the difficulties that arise when complaints are made by one person against another person regarding his or her conduct/behaviour, and to protect the organization in the event that an employee is mistreated, bullied or harassed.

Here are a few examples of the potential cost of not having a code of conduct and clear expectations, derived from actual incidents:

- Employees sacked for having lunch at a strip show (in uniform) – all reinstated as there was no code of conduct or rules to govern where employees should not go in uniform.

- Employee terminated for being under the influence of alcohol was reinstated. Able to prove senior managers often had long lunches and returned to the workplace – lack of consistency. There was no drink/alcohol policy and no code of conduct.

- An Asian woman who did not drink or smoke attended after-work drinks. She was offended by sexual discussions, had smoke blown in her face, her drink was spiked (as a joke) and she was subjected to racial taunts and strong sexual language. Significant financial payout for pain and suffering due to sexual harassment and racial discrimination. No code, no rules, no guidelines regarding drinking at the workplace and no policy on sexual or racial discrimination.

- Pilfering – starts with biros and ends up with the family being supplied with all their school stationery and computer needs.

- Access to the internet – a multitude of cases regarding access to pornographic sites – some won, some lost. A number of otherwise good employees lost through a lack of clear expectations being set out in a code of conduct and being monitored.

Management must ensure that the code is revisited and discussed with employees on a regular basis. It is inevitable that some employees will try to find the loophole or test the boundaries of the code from time to time. A revisit now and again will help remove this tension and give people an opportunity to discuss what is meant by the code.

THE DEVELOPMENT PROCESS – PERFORMANCE STANDARDS

It is difficult to provide generic examples of the development process or the actual performance standards. This is because both the process and the outcomes of the process need to reflect the particular circumstances of the organization. We have, however, provided some examples of performance standards later in this section to give you a feel for what they might look like in practice.

The degree of difficulty involved in the development of performance standards will also vary considerably from organization to organization. At one end of the spectrum are those organizations that already measure carefully and regularly what is going on in their particular processes, as well as the final results, which they usually measure against predetermined targets. If these measures are supported by performance criteria, the standards are complete. You would also expect the team members to already know about these measures, targets and performance standards and to be working to them.

In such organizations, all that is required is a check to ensure that the system by which people are trained on (or learn) these standards is effective. The performance standards themselves must be accurate, up to date and subject to regular review. You must ensure that employees know what the standards are, understand them and are committed to them. If this is not the case, then obviously a review is required, which may lead to a revision in the standards and, in turn, some retraining of team members.

At the other end of the spectrum are those organizations where little is documented; quality assurance is haphazard with standards varying between different groups and individuals – including managers. Fortunately these organizations are fewer and fewer in number and most organizations employing more than 20 people already have some occupational health and safety (OH&S) standards and occasionally some quality standards in place.

The missing link is often those areas of performance that we take for granted, for example productivity/throughput. How many people in your organization have a clear understanding of the work effort/levels of output you expect from them?

In some organizations this will need to be done individually and the documentation will be the job description. We are aware of companies where accountants, lawyers and recruitment consultants are required to bring in two or three times their salary in fees, or in two years they don't have a job. Sales organizations are very conscious of individual sales performance for obvious reasons, but in general we don't see many organizations providing clear expectations to employees in terms of output.

Productivity requirements and quality standards can sometimes seem to be at odds with each other. Many readers would have heard employees lament, 'You told me to slow down to get the quality right, now you tell me to speed up as I am too slow. Make up your mind!' A critical aspect of developing performance standards is having team members (and line managers) understand that it is indeed a balancing act in many work environments to achieve excellent performance. 'Yes, we want you to go slow enough to get the quality right, but as fast as you can without hurting yourself or making a mistake.'

Statements like this can be quite confusing to a team member. Performance standards will, in themselves, not help a lot but the discussion and training and development that accompany the drafting and implementation of performance standards will help develop a better understanding of performance and a greater clarity of expectations at both the individual and team level. In particular, the concept of variance in performance, what actually occurs, why it happens, and what can be done to reduce the degree of variability, are of critical importance.

The process itself

1. Identify the key result areas in the workplace for which you wish to develop performance standards.

2. Establish as many small expert groups as may be necessary to develop and document the standards.

3. Document performance standards for each of the key result areas. (They do not have to be done all at once – prioritize if you need to.)

4. Provide training to employees as part of the roll-out and trial the standards for a reasonable period. Adjust if necessary.

5. Provide regular feedback on employees' performance against the standard.

Note: It is pointless involving people unless they have been deemed to be at least competent, and ideally exceptional, in the area so that they can contribute to the standard development.

Performance standards will take many different forms:

▌ They may be a productivity/throughput standard (x number per hour or day).

▌ They may be in the form of a standard operating procedure (SOP), that is, *Step 1: Set up warning signal and tape off area with hazard tape. Step 2: Ensure emergency escape is usable in the particular circumstances.*

▌ They may be quite generic – *Rework due to quality failure/error < 0.05%.*

SOME EXAMPLES OF PERFORMANCE STANDARDS/CRITERIA

Outcome-based

Productivity/throughput

▎ boxes per hour into store;

▎ services to be completed within 15 minutes of standard service time (refer to manual, p.00);

▎ 45 calls per hour processed in accordance with quality criteria;

▎ minimum class sizes.

Quality

▎ no visible marks on surface (cleanliness);

▎ zero defects;

▎ <0.001% spoilage;

▎ meeting predetermined specifications for presentation of documents/ reports, for example, text noting.

Process-based

Security

All visitors to be given an all-over body check with metal detector on entry and exit.

> ### OH&S
>
> The following equipment shall be worn at all times during this activity – hard hat, goggles, flame-resistant overalls, heat-resistant gloves, work boots.

The format/wording may vary considerably – the key is to ensure employees know what is expected of them and why. Performance standards need to be as few in number as possible to achieve the results required of the particular work group or individual. If there are too many, the system will not work – it has to be simple.

While the performance standards and code of conduct are being developed, the organization needs to prepare its line managers for their coaching role. This is the subject of the next chapter.

It cannot be too strongly emphasized that the line managers, as part of their coaching role, need to ensure that the performance standards are reviewed regularly, according to a plan, and that the commitment to them (evidenced in the level of compliance) is growing rather than diminishing. The way that new employees are recruited and inducted into an organization that has standards and a code of conduct in place will be addressed as part of Chapter 3, which deals with workplace coaching.

Finally, our comment earlier about the importance of clear expectations in dealing with complaints from fellow employees applies equally here. One of the most difficult situations to deal with is where an employee or group of employees consider that the work output or quality of another employee's work is not up to standard.

A comment

Throughout the world we have examples of occupational health and safety disasters arising from inadequate risk management. A natural outcome of risk analysis is a strategy to eliminate or minimize the risk and/or its impact. In many instances these should give rise to the development and implementation of performance standards. The failure to develop such standards after identifying the risks associated with asbestos has lead to significant levels of industrial disease and death, and the consequential litigation costing billions.

Such incidents are commonplace in relation to system failures where performance standards have not been adequately developed or policed (quality, security and environmental, to name a few).

NOTES

1. The Balanced Score Card approach encourages organizations to measure such things as employee and shareholder satisfaction, client/customer satisfaction, environmental performance, contributions to the community and results other than pure financial results.

2. _Gallup Management Journal_, New York, March 15 2001

3

Preparing to coach people

SETTING THE SCENE FOR WORKPLACE COACHING

The traditional role of a line manager in an organization has not included the development/continuous improvement of his or her people. We would be wealthy men if we pocketed a dollar for every time someone on the shop floor or in the workplace complained about the lack of feedback on performance or the lack of opportunity to receive further development, in line with the changes to their job requirements.

Traditional forms of supervision differ from our workplace coaching because these focus on communicating with people only when they 'mess up'. This is not to say that all supervisors in the past operated this way, but in our experience the majority did. This was the industrial policeman-type mentality where people got the feeling they were being watched with a view to catching them out.

It was this environment which led to Frank's chapter, 'From cop to coach: the shop floor supervisor'[1] of the 1990s in *The Return of the Mentor(s)* referred to in the introduction to this book. There were several key messages. Although the story is circa 1993, it was a milestone in improved workplace relationships – a change in the way people work together. Some of these messages were:

▌ If workers saw supervisors in a policing role, interested only in controlling and speaking to them when they got something wrong, the culture would never be a productive one.

▌ Supervisors were not there in the capacity of industrial police but coaches who communicate and consult with the work team – working together to continuously improve and enjoy work.

▌ The word 'supervisor' was an out-of-date term; rather, it was the line manager or team leader who is the human face of the organization, presenting that clear link with the people who actually do the work.

▌ Team leaders were facilitators who assisted the work group through greater involvement and ownership. A facilitation role built on workplace coaching. (People who see supervision as supervising a process to get an output, forget that it is the people who keep this happening day after day.)

These messages really demonstrate how inappropriate a word like 'supervisor' is. We have always preferred 'line manager' or 'team leader'. These are the people who facilitate the role of the work team. They must be the coaches and mentors of the work team from the time they enter the workplace, and over their time at the organization.

Further messages are clearly focused on the need for a line manager to move outside what has been the traditional role and incorporate the role of a workplace coach. Before looking in detail at what makes a good workplace coach, we need to confirm the importance of having the right people as line managers (and coaches) and having the right team members to coach.

This raises a critical aspect of team performance. How does a new member get to be selected to join the team? Who selects the new team member? We have heard line managers many times respond to questions about an under-performing person – 'Well, I didn't pick them!' It is the job of the line manager to hire his or her team. It involves selection, recruitment and retention. The clear objective is to hire people who perform to the standards and will conduct themselves in ways that contribute to a safe, healthy, enjoyable and harassment-free workplace. It is about asking each individual member of the team to become his or her own policeman and to watch over his or her own performance and behaviour.

We suspect there is not a line manager reading these words who has not at some time recruited a person whom they thought was right for the job, and realized later they had made a mistake (sometimes a monumental one) either in terms of cost, irreparable damage to the way the team works together, or both. We pick this up in Chapter 7 from a different perspective – moving from coaching to discipline.

If we had a magic solution to deal with this problem we would spend our entire waking lives letting people into the secret. The bottom line is, there is no foolproof way of ensuring you get the right person. However, by clearly specifying our expectations of team members, the risk of error in selection can be greatly reduced. One aspect of the specification should be that the person is keen, has a thirst for learning and a commitment to helping others.

It is our view, whether we are dealing with an established business or one which is new, the process supporting selection and recruitment is the same. The starting points are: *how is the job designed* and *how will the work be organized?*

We stress again, it is not our intention to turn you into a recruitment specialist, but to introduce you briefly to a process that will help you to adopt your rightful role in being involved in determining who will become a member of your team and the expectations to be met.

Teams

Before we move on, we need to say something about teams. The word 'teams' has probably been done to death over the last 10 to 15 years, but we honestly can't find anything to replace it. One aspect of teams that is seldom made clear in discussions is the different types of teams and how team behaviour will need to vary to fit the particular type of team.

Many people only think of teams as a typical sporting team – a coach (who may also be captain) who we would call a line manager, and a group of players, all available to play the same game (albeit with different but contributory roles). The fact is, every team is different! You cannot simply apply one set of principles to the multitude of different teams. You need to form the most appropriate team for a particular workplace and then adopt other systems to fit that team model.

We do not propose to go into this in great depth here, but present a couple of examples. First, there is the type of team described above such as a golf team (for example, Ryder Cup), or tennis team (Davis Cup) in which the players may practise together, discuss their performances and help each other, but actually play the game as an individual, or in the case of doubles, a pair. Where this type of team occurs in the workplace, it needs to have a purpose-built method of operation. The other 'team', which is often not seen as a team as such, is the hierarchical team made up of different levels of managers. There is no reason why it can't operate as a team – it just means that there has to be some adaptation. The important thing here is that workplace coaching can operate in any team of any type – it simply requires some adjustment to meet the particular circumstances of the organization.

JOB DESIGN/WORK ORGANIZATION

The examination of the work process should allow you to determine what will be required of team members to achieve the work outcomes needed to meet the performance standards and code of conduct. There is considerable evidence to suggest organizations fail to consider job design or work reorganization as a vacancy arises – consequently missing frequent opportunities to streamline and continuously improve the way work is done. When this occurs, a reassessment needs to be undertaken.

The determination of the extent of multi-skilling versus specialization, the number of people needed, the technology that may be available to improve the way work is done, are not often considered. The response is more often, 'The assistant accountant has resigned – you had better advertise the job.'

The role of the workplace coach should require a more active role in getting the right people on your team by:

I reviewing job descriptions;

I specifying the type of person you need to take on the job (therefore reducing the chances of a mismatch occurring);

I selecting people based on demonstrated ability or potential to perform to the standard the organization expects, not on what they have or have not done (or say they have done);

I ensuring the code of conduct is clearly stated and communicated during the selection process;

I assessing applicants' responses to the code of conduct through 'what if' scenarios (here you do not want nodding responses to advice on, say, sexual harassment or zero tolerance on drugs; rather what will or won't be accepted. This clarity of expectations has often caused an applicant to withdraw);

I assessing applicants' commitment to learning and to providing assistance to other team members.

The key to this process is to elicit views from applicants up front about their work ethic and their idea of how a workplace should function, prior to receiving responses to specific questions.

PERFORMANCE-BASED SELECTION

Equally important as the communication of the code of conduct to potential applicants, is the communication of the performance standards that apply to work and the nature of the job itself – particularly the difficult or unpleasant parts.

In many of the organizations we work with, it has become commonplace to double interview (even for lower level jobs). The first interview is to reduce the numbers; then some quality time can be spent with the remaining applicants, seeking responses to performance expectations and, where practicable, to set tasks that assess competence and confidence in meeting the specified standards. For many jobs, the best criterion for selection is to ask applicants to demonstrate their capabilities and then assess their performance accordingly.

Where setting practical tasks is impossible or inappropriate, such as with higher level positions or for health and safety reasons, a series of case studies, scenarios or in-basket activities can provide considerable insight into the ability and/or potential of applicants to meet expectations. For example, teachers should be asked to take classes of full duration based on typical student groups.

The debrief of such activities/selection techniques is critical, as it also provides the applicant with a good 'feel' for whether he or she can handle the job. For example, the applicant may well decide this is not the job he or she wants to do, or the organization is not one he or she wants to work for. Better to find out then rather than later. Unfortunately, many organizations rely entirely on an interview and referee reports to make their selection. It is worth bearing in mind that people do misrepresent themselves at selection interviews.

A comment

There are some classic tales of people gaining employment under false pretences. For example, there was a deputy general manager who gave a referee for a job he had never held, and an academic who was appointed Head of School based on postgraduate qualifications he had never completed. The most common mistakes are contacting only the referees provided and not checking with other previous employers or other records. The results can be frightening. We have come across an accountant who had been in prison for embezzlement; a supervisor who had been sacked from three meat works for bullying and assault; a senior manager with several psychiatric problems; and a convicted paedophile appointed as head of a child care centre.

In summary, we emphasize that the coach must be involved in the selection and recruitment of people for his or her team. Successful recruitment requires both a job description (including a company profile) and a person specification.

INDUCTION

To be a successful member of a team requires a thorough induction to the workplace, the team and the organization. It is during the first few hours, days and months that the employee relationship is established (ideally with little ambiguity). It is the time when principles and practice of performance feedback are embedded. It is also the time when it becomes clear to new personnel that it is a major objective of the organization to continuously prepare, plan and deliver on learning needs to maximize performance and individual competence. Team members must also be encouraged to take responsibility for their own learning.

Any induction should include a formal introduction to coaching and/or mentoring as a part of the organization's everyday working life. Workplace coaching begins from day one.

Finally, probation must be part of those early days of exposure. This is where new team members are brought into contact with performance standards and the code of conduct for the first time. It is essential that the probation period be based on a development plan.

Through what E Wight Bakke[2] called a 'fusion' process the principles and practice of performance feedback, based on early intervention (and in relation to excellent performance or underperformance), are made absolutely clear. This is where continuous feedback is based on 'no surprises' as part and parcel of the way the teams function. This is also where linkages are made to how the induction tools are used by the workplace coach to determine any training and development needs for the individual and the team, and how plans to do so are developed, implemented and measured for success.

In summary, we see workplace coaching as an interpersonal approach by a manager or team leader to continuously improve the capability and/or conduct of both the individual and the team.

WHAT IS A WORKPLACE COACH?

Workplace coaching is the cornerstone of our approach to people management. Anyone who wants to be a competent coach, and is prepared to develop some basic skills, can be a competent coach. Right now you are probably asking yourself, what is required for a coach to be successful? How do we select and train those people we believe to have the potential to carry out the role? Clearly there is no magic formula for selecting coaches; it depends on the game you are playing. Some great coaches have been great players, but then many great players have failed as coaches. High technical ability may be an asset or it may be a liability.

Many of you would argue that a good coach is above all a good communicator. A good communicator is one who can deliver a message clearly and simply, is a good, active, empathetic listener and behaves in a manner that is consistent with the message that is being delivered. A role model!

The line manager is a workplace coach who will survive on his or her capability to be consistent in words and action – people saying one thing but doing something different will guarantee negativity and ultimately failure. Many of us have seen these double standards and corruption in the community and workplace generally. We must ensure we do not have corrupt coaches – coaches with double standards will fail. A coach must have a mental toughness, the courage of his or her conviction and be credible. The simple message is: both words and action are critical to success.

Workplace coaching is about developing trust between all members of the team and an understanding that regular day-to-day feedback will be provided in a way that is valid, reliable, consistent and fair. Trust will allow an acceptance that all team members can expect to be told, in a non-threatening way, when they are performing excellently or when they are underperforming.

When we have worked with companies in identifying the features of an excellent coach, a broad canvas is painted. They say an excellent coach must be an active listener; be respected (not necessarily liked) by team members as a professional (have integrity and honesty, be patient and direct); be supportive but provide freedom to initiate; be a role model and a setter of standards, using a supportive approach to mistakes, yet using mistakes as a learning opportunity.

These companies say a coach must also be an accurate observer of work activities. Not observation by spying, but timing his or her presence in the workplace to ensure team members know that the emphasis is more an interest in and enthusiasm for what is going on whilst being there to assist if necessary. 'You cannot expect to know what is going on if you are not in the street every day'. This means being involved in the daily work of the workplace; being alongside, not over.

Familiarity or friendship are not prerequisites to being an effective coach. In many ways coaches, like teachers, should have a sense of vocation. They are born, not made. However, with training and feedback, we can make them better teachers and coaches. To be successful, both the words and the action are critical.

We now turn to a process for developing coaches to be both competent and confident. People who are able to set the mood, tone and behaviour for coaching in the workplace and then do it in a way which demonstrates their actions, are both consistent and sustainable. They demonstrate success for all team members and ultimately the organization.

Workplace coaching activities

We see coaching as continuous personal interaction and (where required) intervention in the team's activities, to lift, sustain and improve the performance of the individual and the team. Intervention for the purposes of coaching may occur at any time, but particularly when a coach detects excellent performance or underperformance. Intervention may take the form of encouragement, recognition, praise, advice, demonstration, training or any other form of learning to improve competence or behaviour. It can also focus on building confidence, which supports performance.

We use the words 'workplace coaching' to describe a set of interrelated activities:

- clarifying expectations;

- providing feedback in the workplace as close to the event as possible (early intervention);

- making coaching part of the line manager's style of dealing with members of his or her work team;

- making the workplace more comfortable and satisfactory for team members so that they can accept both positive and negative feedback in the spirit of coaching – we are here not only to achieve excellent results but to enjoy our work and interaction with other team members;

- targeting areas where performance or behaviour need to be improved and then acting by developing plans to improve individual or team performance and/or to recognize excellent performance (this must include follow-up and assessment of outcomes/results).

You may recall that Figure 1.1 (see page 17) stressed the importance of making sure that the expectations and standards for performance are made clear and abided by across the entire work team. These expectations provide the criteria against which excellence or underperformance can be judged.

For workplace coaching to move from the specification of performance to an interactive process in the workplace where the line manager provides day-to-day feedback, a clear set of principles needs to be established to guide all line managers. These will include performance and behaviour.

These principles, like expectations, must be agreed to and a commitment made to abide by them. We issue a strong warning – just as finger prints and snow flakes are all different, so too are organizations. A set of principles for one organization may not work so well for another. Organizations should develop their own set of principles with the involvement of senior managers and line managers.

Principles of workplace coaching

The list below is not a single recipe for success but a sample from organizations we have worked with that have accepted workplace coaching as the driving force of managing people. The list provides line managers with the basis for a set of rules within which successful coaching can occur.

WORKPLACE COACHING SHOULD:

I provide for regular day-to-day, on the job feedback based on early intervention;

I provide for genuine two-way feedback (coach to team member – member to coach);

I provide encouragement;

I have formal criteria (established and agreed expectations) for measuring performance and behaviour;

I observe and confirm excellent performance;

I include various ways of providing feedback;

I be relevant for each individual;

I link individual goals to team and organizational goals;

I be simple and practical with minimum paperwork;

I be cost/time effective;

I have no surprises;

■ emphasize continuous improvement;

■ identify and deliver the development needs of individuals and teams.

This may look like a list of 'motherhood' statements, but really they are guiding principles as to how coaches will operate within the organization. To embed these principles, the environment within which they are to be applied must be transparent.

Taking stock

We have so far stressed the importance of line managers seeing themselves as coaches who facilitate the activities of work teams through clear and simple communication based on continuous feedback for both excellence and underperformance. Coaches work within a culture each helped to make, based on respect and integrity (but are not necessarily liked).

Workplace coaching must include the provision of feedback within an environment that is comfortable and satisfactory for all. Above all, workplace coaching must focus on the continuous pursuit of improvement based on clear and deliverable development plans, which are monitored.

All workplace coaches must have been involved in, agreed to and committed to a set of guiding principles. These principles will be different for each organization. What is not different is that the feedback activities will fall into two different but interlinked environments – inside the workplace (on the job) and outside the workplace (during a formal review). Outside the workplace can be any suitable venue which is private, relatively quiet and free from unnecessary interruption. Both are important, both have their place, but it is the feedback inside the workplace which builds the foundation for any feedback outside the workplace during the formal review – time out to sit down and discuss performance and behaviour.

The model in Figure 3.1 provides an overview of the key features of each: who is involved (coach, individual, team), when (close to the event, before or after an event), when again (present time, past), what (practical/operational, strategic/tactical), where (in the workplace, away from the work site).

An explanation of how each is applied is the focus of the next two chapters, which deal with how to do it, taking the principles of workplace coaching and doing it under operational conditions.

Off the job – outside the workplace (During a formal review)	On the job – inside the workplace (During work activities)
· With individual and team	· With the individual
· Before and after an 'event'	· Close to the 'event'
· It is 'reflective' (past performance)	· It is now (present time)

· It is both strategic and tactical (future)
  - where do we want to be in six months?
  - what plan do we need to improve?
	· It is tactical/operational
	  - it is 'now' time – today
	  - supported by follow-up outside the
	    workplace

· Reinforcement	· Early intervention
· Defining standards/expectations	· Incident/event based
· Planning how to improve	· Praising excellent performance
· Implementing plan	

Figure 3.1   Overview of off the job/on the job feedback

NOTES

1. Remember that the word 'supervisor' literally means 'watching over'. One of the interesting aspects of this terminology, 'from cop to coach' is that it is actually out of date. Police in many parts of the world, whilst still carrying out their traditional role of monitoring the community for compliance with the law, have moved to community policing – in a sense, doing some coaching, trying to prevent breaches of the law and helping those people/communities who need some assistance to develop a culture of compliance.

2. E Wight Bakke papers, 1929–71 (bulk 1945–70) #5960, Kheel Center for Labor-Management Documentation and Archives, Cornell University Library.

4

Operating as a coach on the job

On the job (inside the workplace during work activities) is on the shop floor, maintaining day-to-day contact with the team whilst they work. It means acting in a way that demonstrates interest and enthusiasm, with an eye and ear for excellent performance and for assisting each individual in a productive way where underperformance is noted and acted upon. It is about building relationships; bringing employees up to excellence with a clear realization that the coach has an inspirational role.

This is where evidence of performance has its origins – where early intervention (as close in time to the event as possible) takes place. Early intervention allows for the provision of immediate feedback. Feedback is of an informal type, so when it moves to the formal review, there are no surprises. Although informal, two-way feedback provided on the job develops trust in a powerful way.

Two-way feedback is not about the watcher (line manager) acting alone. It may be, but must be based on encouraging employees to ask or check if something is right or wrong. It should include opportunities for reassurance from a friendly ear – more important, to include opportunities to recommend.

Irrespective of whether feedback is given informally through on the job interaction or off the job during a formal review, it must be based on the following principles:

- be linked to specific observed behaviour;

- be descriptive not judgemental;

- be limited and focused, not overwhelming;

- be two-way, based on questions and discussions;

- be focused on performance, not personality;

- be conclusive with prescriptive outcomes;

- be presented in a professional way.

We need to be a little more specific about what the coach provides feedback on. Feedback should relate to competence to do the job to a standard, particularly in relation to safety, regulatory or environmental requirements (see performance standards examples, Chapter 2).

This may involve an employee not using a piece of equipment correctly, taking short cuts in a procedure, failing to assess the risks of a job before commencing, failing to wear protective equipment, dealing with a customer in an unacceptable manner, or failing to take account of individual differences when in a teaching or training situation.

Feedback might also relate to behaviour in terms of a code of conduct. For example:

- time management (punctuality, return from breaks);

- attendance (time off);

- team relationships (respectful towards others);

- procedures for leaving the work station;

- commencing and finishing classes on time.

(See code of conduct examples, Chapter 2.) In some cases it might be a combination of competence and behaviour.

Feedback must also relate to excellent performance. Feedback that tells people they have done excellently is crucial. It is our experience that most people only receive feedback when they make errors. This form of feedback is rarely supported by a demonstration of how it should have been done or what will be done to ensure it does not happen again. We must all try to give more positive feedback.

PROVIDING INFORMAL FEEDBACK ON THE JOB

We promote and use a very simple approach to the provision of informal feedback. We call it 'GIDAY'. Figure 4.1 explains what GIDAY is and how it is used for both acknowledging excellent performance and dealing with underperformance. Of course the model is designed to show the process; the manner in which it is applied and the language used depends on the workplace; we believe the simpler the better, but again, with professionalism.

Informal on the job – feedback process ★ Acknowledging excellence ★	Informal on the job – coaching process ★ Targeting improvement ★
Greeting · 'Good day', 'Hello Bob! How are you?'	**G**reeting · 'Good day', 'Hello Bob! How are you?'
Identify excellence · 'That is great work – how did you do that?'	**I**dentify the issue · Describe non-compliance clearly · Relate to work standards
Discuss · Encourage team member to explain what they have done · Two-way – listen · Confirm benefits	**D**iscuss · Two-way – gain a response · Seek an explanation
Agree · Reinforce excellent work · 'Keep it up' – commit to tell others	**A**gree · Confirm standard expected · Gain commitment to change
Yes · Follow up and confirm excellent work and benefits with others · Yes, it is important to tell others! · Make a note	**Y**es · Follow up and check practice maintains standard · Take further action if required · Yes, it is important to act on under-performance! · Make a note

Figure 4.1   Approach to the provision of informal feedback

KEY FEATURES

Acknowledging excellence

If you have difficulty in looking employees in the eye and telling them they have done well, you share a common problem. We have found the majority of line managers are uncomfortable with it. It is therefore one of the major emphases in our training of coaches.

Really, the bullet points under each step in Figure 4.1 say it all, but we must emphasize how important it is to shift from a commitment to tell all the other team members, to actually doing it when they are all together. It must be timely to have impact and meaning. 'Yes, I will follow up on excellent performance' or, 'Yes, I will follow up on the need for improvement.'

Targeting improvement

If you have difficulty looking employees in the eye and telling them they are not complying with a standard, then you had better overcome it. Any non-compliance with performance standards or code of conduct must be dealt with immediately. Here both the 'agree' and 'follow-up' stages are critical. 'Yes, I will follow up on underperformance!'

If the non-compliance is to do with competence, the coach might be able to deal with it by demonstration, practice and drill, or call on a job specialist to do so. This may require a coaching plan that clearly sets out what has to be learnt and how what is learnt will be assessed. In terms of behaviour, the non-compliance might be to do with punctuality. This can be dealt with by a simple discussion, clear evidence provided by the coach, an opportunity for the employee to explain – then a commitment to improve by the employee, or recognition of assistance and action required by the coach.

Whatever the non-compliance, there must be a two-way conversation, followed by a commitment to change from the employee ('Yes, I will fix it'). More important, there has to be a commitment from the coach to follow up and implement the necessary action to improve performance. The follow-up will also involve the coach checking subsequent practice by the employee to ensure the agreed standard is maintained. At times it will be necessary for periods of consolidation to accompany any coaching on the job.

It is important to reinforce one of the key principles of workplace coaching: genuine two-way feedback must be just that. It is pointless to have a work environment in which the coach is the only person who does the observing and talking.

We suggest that a good starting point is a work environment that encourages all team members to have a say on how:

▮ work ought to be done;

▮ learning should take place;

▮ problems should be dealt with;

▮ work can be improved.

Of course such an environment must be managed well in terms of the right mix of discipline and freedom to initiate.

Creating an environment for both the team and the individual to motivate themselves, builds confidence and helps them to overcome obstacles. This is about building team work and the line manager demonstrating leadership. This in itself creates confidence to raise issues, concerns and work improvement, so that when the coach finds it necessary to intervene, both points of view are expressed and all facts are brought out. This must apply in respect to both excellent and underperformance.

This simple technique may be all that is required of the coach. However, in the event of subsequent non-compliance or a lack of time to deal with non-compliance in detail, it may be necessary to deal with it during a formal review process, or, depending on the seriousness of the non-compliance, transferred to the discipline process (see Chapter 7). This is dealt with through coaching off the job (see Chapter 5). It might also require the formal assessment of the employee's competence by a trained and competent assessor. The outcomes of the assessment will confirm the level of the employee's competence and, if necessary, what improvement is required.

Irrespective of where coaching takes place, evidence of excellence or underperformance becomes critical. Any judgement must be based on the quality and integrity of the evidence against predetermined standards.

THE QUALITY AND INTEGRITY OF EVIDENCE

In providing feedback on human performance, there is nothing more important than evidence. Some of you reading this will have worked in organizations where the feedback from your supervisor/manager was based on subjectivity, like whether you:

▮ drank with the boss after work;

▮ were a member of the same community group as your boss;

▮ followed the same sporting club or interest as the boss;

▮ did as you were told.

Many of the criteria (if they could be called that) had nothing to do with your performance on the job.

Evidence used in the assessment of a person's performance will never have any value or acceptance unless it is:

- *Objective* – related to the competence and behaviour of the person – not whether you like them (free of discrimination).

- *Valid* – judgements relate directly to the agreed standards of competence and code of conduct required to do the job.

- *Reliable* – the evidence can be trusted and preferably supported by more than one source.

- *Fair* – an employee will be given the opportunity to dispute the evidence and/or explain the circumstances of the event.

- *Consistent* – the coach will be consistent in his or her behaviour in collecting evidence and operating as coach both on and off the job.

- *Transparent* – the process for collecting evidence and making judgements is clear to all employees. There are no hidden agendas. The criteria by which the coach operates are clearly known to all.

- *Result-focused* – evidence gathered will reward excellent performance and provide clear and agreed plans of action to improve underperformance.

- *Clearly recorded* – noted on the back of a coach's hand, in a notebook, on an electronic diary – as long as it is clear and provides sufficient detail.

Taking stock again

Since we last took stock on page 50, we have moved from the principles of workplace coaching to their application. We promote their application informally, on the job, using our 'GIDAY' process, or off the job through a formal review.

Before we move on to an explanation of how we apply the coaching principles through feedback in a formal review, we want to reinforce our message that managing performance is about continuous improvement based on providing regular day-to-day feedback and coaching as close in time to the event as possible (early intervention). In doing this, the line manager acknowledges excellent performance and targets and responds to underperformance in a planned and achievable way. We stress the importance of:

- genuine two-way feedback;

- early intervention;

- recognition of excellent performance;

- objective evidence of non-compliance;

- development, delivery, review and measurement of individual and team development needs.

We acknowledge here that workplace coaches cannot spend all of their time on the job (inside the workplace). Neither can all that is required to provide informal feedback on excellent or underperformance be dealt with there. There will always be a need to follow up through a formal feedback session away from the work activity (off the job).

The key to all of this is early intervention. It can bring some real success and a lack of it can result in a disaster.

CASE STUDY – SUCCESS

A manager, unimpressed by the performance (mistakes/sloppy work) and attitude of an employee (grumpy/unhappy) at the time of taking up a new position, decides to intervene. Within a week he has a meeting with the employee. The general expectation is that the employee will be dismissed. The employee raises the following points:

❙ bored – not enough work;

❙ poor environment;

❙ out-of-date technology;

❙ no induction/no training/no explanation of work to be carried out;

❙ feels isolated – would like to leave.

A performance improvement plan was agreed, with additional duties, new technology and training/monitoring put in place. The change/improvement was immediate.

Result	5 years	doubles salary
	10 years	head hunted as top performer in field

CASE STUDY – FAILURE

An employee has been verbally abusing fellow workers for years. There is no code of conduct, no guidelines. A new supervisor notices the rapid turnover of staff and asks some new employees why they are leaving. 'X is constantly in your face, swearing at you, telling you you're useless. You just get sick of it.' When reported to senior management, the response is 'X is always like that, tell them to ignore it.'

After four more incidents, action is taken against X. X goes on stress leave – doesn't return, there is a considerable payout, lots of potentially good employees are lost, and it adds to the reputation of a 'nasty work-place' at considerable cost to the employer. Oh for early intervention!

5

Operating as a coach during a formal review

Off the job (outside the workplace) can be anywhere that provides a quiet, confidential environment. This is where the formal review takes place with each member of the team. There are some major considerations here in relation to the likely behaviour of the employee during the review.

It is important to consider the likely impact on each employee when they are taken out of their familiar and comfortable environment to one which is unfamiliar, and for some, perhaps frightening. Based on previous experience or simply fear of the unknown, employees often display signs of:

  ▌ distress;

  ▌ fear; or

  ▌ lack of trust.

Employees these days often convince themselves they are in trouble or are about to be made redundant. Many will find it difficult to accept that the review is a regular part of people management aimed at telling them formally how they are doing, how they can improve and reaching agreement on what assistance they will be given to improve and/or continue their individual development.

Each employee must receive feedback that is directly related to their performance and behaviour in meeting clearly defined expectations. The feedback provided will be in relation to excellent performance and under-performance – and guess what? There will be no surprises. The line manager will be using objective evidence that has been gathered from direct observation of both performance and behaviour on the job (in the workplace).

In operating off the job, the coach is reflecting with each team member on past performance. We have said much about the importance of evidence: to have any value, the coach must structure the evidence so that it is directly related to expectations.

Not all of the evidence needed to provide feedback on excellence or underperformance can be obtained by the coach moving day-to-day amongst the team whilst they work. Depending on the size of the organization and the scope of work activities (for example across shift), it may be necessary to consult with other line managers and to access attendance or other records. We say this evidence needs to be introduced in a particular way and relates directly to how the whole practice of performance feedback is introduced to the organization.

Figure 1.1, page 17, sets out the people management process, and lists four key features:

1. managing;

2. people;

3. performance;

4. development.

The first feature includes communication, which is about making sure every-one knows what is involved. This is where the role of the coach (line manager) must be made totally clear, in particular that the coach will operate on the job through constant informal reviews of performance, and off the job through a formal review process.

It must also be made clear that evidence of excellence and underperfor-mance will be gathered progressively, based on interaction between the coach and all team members so that there will be no surprises. It must also be made clear that, in preparation for the formal review, evidence may come to light through objective means which the coach has not been able to raise with the team member directly. Our approach to dealing with this is that the first formal review is a benchmark review where the coach is clearly able to con-firm judgements based on evidence already raised with the team member and, where new evidence is raised, it is set to one side for the moment. The coach might say, 'Jack, on reviewing your performance in readiness for this review, I have confirmed you were absent on the following days. In view of our policy of no surprises, all we will do is discuss it and note it down as an area we will formally review in, say, six months.'[1]

Taking stock

We have said that a formal review is the process by which the coach provides feedback off the job (outside the workplace). Whilst we argue always that there should be no surprises during the formal feedback process, we also accept there may be! To respond, we say the employee must be given a fair go. The formal review process should begin with a 'benchmark' review where no final judgement is made on any new evidence of underperformance (or non-compliance to a code of conduct) introduced at that time. Through discussion, expectations can be reinforced and agreement reached that this particular underperformance (or bad behaviour) will be revisited at the next formal review, for which a timeframe needs to be established.

All formal reviews will focus on:

- Where are we now?
- Where do we want to be in six months?
- What plan do we need to improve?
- What other form of individual development should be considered?
- Implementing the improvement plan.
- Monitoring the progress of the improvement plan.

The conduct of a formal review is challenging: it requires attention to detail, total clarity in the evidence to be discussed, and needs to be carefully planned. To have any value, a review must be structured and presented in a logical sequence. The extent to which this happens is directly related to how well the evidence has been gathered and documented in the first place. Depending on the organization, we urge you to consider something we have learnt over the years: blue-collar workers, children and dogs can smell a phoney a mile off!

PROVIDING FORMAL FEEDBACK OFF THE JOB

Whilst it is not always essential, we generally recommend commencing formal feedback through a benchmark review. What then follows is a structured process that can be used for that purpose or the regular reviews that follow.

A decision on the minimum number of formal reviews should be made during the planning component of phase 1 (see Chapter 1, pages 17–18). The key is that the frequency should be driven by the extent of underperformance of the employee. We have put in systems where the poorer performers are on fortnightly reviews, the better on six-monthly reviews.

The approach we will describe for providing formal feedback off the job is just one example of how it might be done. It will focus on examples of key activities on which feedback can be given, and can be adjusted, extended and customized for any organization, depending on the nature of the work. There can be combinations, but whatever approach is used it must relate to expectations in terms of performance standards and the code of conduct.

Before describing the approach, it is important to realize that not every area of competence required to perform a job can or should be listed. The feedback package of activities should be in clusters; for example, performance on the job covering:

- approach to tasks;
- execution of tasks;
- tools and equipment reliability;
- personal safety.

Alternatively, as another example:

- job planning;
- performance focus;
- occupational health and safety;
- operation of equipment;
- managing learning;
- designing assessment.

What is important is that it is a 'big picture' review, which must focus on all major areas of performance and behaviour. Our structure consists of two components, A and B.

Component A, Designing a structure for a formal review (feedback), consists of five steps, which deal with:

1. Determining the areas of competence and behaviour that feedback will be given on.

2. Indicators of performance.

3. The importance of rating scales.

4. Marking the rating scale.

5. Writing comments.

Component B, Conducting a formal review, consists of six steps, which deal with:

1. Planning the feedback session.

2. Preparing emotionally for the feedback session.

3. Conducting the feedback session.

4. Reaching an agreed result.

5. Recording the outcomes of the feedback session and planning continuous improvement activities.

6. Monitoring and evaluating the continuous improvement activities.

A: DESIGNING A STRUCTURE FOR A FORMAL REVIEW (FEEDBACK)

The importance of involving representatives of all key players has already been stressed. We would also stress the importance of validating all of the work produced.

Step 1. Determining the areas of competence and behaviour that feedback will be given on

These must relate to expectations. Some examples might be:

▌ job planning;

▌ time management (this is used as an example through Steps 2 to 5);

▌ communication;

▌ continuous improvement;

▌ occupational health and safety;

▌ equipment operation;

- teamwork;
- learning assessment and design;
- learner management.

These will vary in relation to the breadth and complexity of the work area (customer service and customer relations would be included for many jobs and organizations). We should make the point that the development of the performance criteria to be applied in respect of these expectations needs to be determined in the context of the organization. What sounds or looks subjective in one organization might be precisely what another organization wants (for example, works flexibly – moves between jobs as required).

Step 2. Indicators of performance

Write an over-arching statement that describes what is expected of employees in managing their time.

Time management

Makes most productive use of time by planning, working flexibly and working to job completion.

Step 3. The importance of rating scales

List the criteria (indicators of performance/expectations) on which evidence will be gathered and judgements will be made on compliance.

Time management

Makes most productive use of time by planning, working flexibly and working to job completion.

Indicators of performance

- Returns to task promptly after planned/unplanned breaks in work.
- Plans work – establishes priorities.
- At work station ready to commence before scheduled start time.
- Continues working until relieved in continuous work environment.
- Works flexibly (moving between jobs if required).

The coach must be totally clear about what evidence is required to apply these criteria.

Note: These indicators can be adjusted to suit the job and the organization.

Step 4. Marking the rating scale

This requires a rating scale that clearly indicates the extent to which the criteria (indicators of performance) have been met. Here is an example:

It is critical the rating scale is clear and unambiguous. The rating scale should also be accompanied by a comments section, in which the coach can summarize his or her judgement of the employee. More is said on comments in Step 5.

There is a necessity with any rating system to facilitate 'moderation' meetings from time to time for coaches to compare notes on how the rating scale is being applied. This moderation process needs to be included in the basic training for workplace coaches.

Time management

Makes most productive use of time by planning, working flexibly and working to job completion.

Does not always meet expectations	Always meets expectations	Exceeds expectations

Comments

....

....

....

Indicators of performance

- Returns to tasks promptly after planned/unplanned breaks in work.
- Plans work – establishes priorities.
- At work station ready to commence before scheduled start time.
- Continues working until relieved in continuous work environment.
- Works flexibly (moving between jobs if required).

Step 5. Writing comments

The comments section should contain:

▌ examples of evidence in relation to either excellence or underperformance with dates and times if required;

▌ notes for reinforcing the expectations for this performance;

▌ points for discussion and agreement as to how underperformance can be dealt with;

▌ a preliminary plan for performance improvement.

The importance of the rating scale

The clarity of the rating scale in relation to expectations (indicators of performance) cannot be over-emphasized. It is here much of the good work can be undone through rating scales that are subjective and far too open to bias or ambiguity.

A poorly designed rating scale can have a major impact on an employee's confidence. It can also lead to aggression, anger, downright rebellion or, worse, a refusal to participate by the workforce. An effective way of demonstrating a rating scale that is a serious worry and likely to find little support and a backlash, is through a contrived example.

Time management

Maintains punctuality and makes best use of time to plan work.

Negative indicators:

- job takes too long
- job site is left in a mess

Positive indicators:

- makes best use of available time
- is ready for work at start time

Areas for concern

You might like to make your own observations before moving on. Our concerns are:

- The criteria used for both negative and positive indicators are too brief.

- What is the difference between a rating of 1, 2, 3, 4 or 5 – for example, what are the degrees of compliance expectations?

- What does a 3 mean?

- The potential for employees to walk around the workplace talking in numbers about their own performance.

- Of even greater concern, employees asking their team mate, 'I am a 3½, what are you?'

Marking the rating scale

Anyone involved in assessment will tell you that you must be totally clear on, a) the criteria you are using as evidence to confirm compliance to performance standards and code of conduct; and b) the evidence you have to confirm either excellence or underperformance.

The coach conducting the formal review must be totally sure of what the review requires, the evidence collected, and compliance or non-compliance with the indicators of performance. These things need to be in place before making a judgement on the extent to which an employee:

- does not always meet expectations;

- always meets expectations;

- exceeds expectations.

The coach must have no doubts – but be prepared to discuss matters openly with the employee. In some instances there may be insufficient evidence available to make a judgement. Once again, this is exactly why a benchmark review is important. The coach may have to say, 'Jack, I haven't seen enough of you to rate you in this area – so I will hold it over until our next review'.

Taking stock again

Since we last took stock we have discussed the role of the coach in providing feedback off the job (outside the workplace), in the first instance through a formal benchmark review. In many ways, this is a pilot or trial run to introduce the activity and ensure validity, reliability, consistency, transparency and acceptance of the process. Everyone involved in having a formal review of their performance must be very clear on what it is intended to achieve, and how it will be managed by the coach.

We provided guidelines for constructing a formal review package; in particular how work expectations can be documented, and how each employee will be rated against the criteria (indicators of performance) applicable to the expectations.

PREPARING FOR A FORMAL REVIEW

Before we move on to how the coach will conduct the formal review, there are a number of important links that need to be made from the design of the formal review package to its implementation.

One link is the importance of the coach providing every team member with a copy of the review package relevant to their job. Each employee must have sufficient time to once again familiarize themselves and to also rate themselves in relation to each of the expectations contained in the package. This is an imperative as it will ensure plenty of healthy discussion during the review. More importantly, it will ensure an interactive two-way review. Obviously the package should reflect the level and type of work being performed, and be as simple as possible.

The coach will find that some employees do not rate themselves highly and will be pleasantly surprised by the coach's judgement. On the other hand, a smaller number will see themselves operating at a higher rating. In either case, particularly the second, it requires the coach to be totally prepared.

The second link involves who should attend the formal review besides the coach and the employee. In many ways this is a strong test of how well the entire people management process has been introduced. Where there is suspicion or doubt on the part of the employees, they may ask their representatives to be involved.

From an individual employee point of view and regardless of whether unions are involved or not, the importance of involving the one-up manager cannot be overstated. In other words, to ensure fairness and even-handedness, an employee who knows that his or her manager's manager is an active participant in the process will be much more confident about the outcomes than if he or she thinks the judgements are purely the views of one person.

Another factor will be the competence and integrity of the coach. Reviewing an employee's performance requires a broad range of skills. Some of these are the competence and confidence of the coach to:

▌ communicate clearly;

▌ listen actively;

▌ observe thoroughly;

- handle difficult employees;

- manage conflict (in some cases);

- deal in facts;

- set realistic goals;

- support but provide team members with the freedom to initiate;

- turn mistakes into learning activities;

- act with honesty, integrity and patience (professionalism);

- build confidence;

- assist team members to overcome obstacles;

- facilitate learning and, where able, impart competence;

- create an environment for the team to motivate themselves;

- assist in continuous individual development.

Right now you are probably thinking, 'I've never met a line manager with all those attributes.' Neither have we, but this is our target! Also, of course, not all of these are necessarily used during a formal review and there are probably other attributes that are relevant.

The most important thing is that all coaches involved in the management of people are thoroughly prepared. This will include how to coach and provide informal feedback on the job using GIDAY, and how to coach and provide formal feedback off the job through a formal review. We deal with this later in the chapter.

In our experience senior managers generally believe their line managers are very good communicators and have the prerequisite competences to be a good workplace coach. Regrettably this is seldom accurate, hence the need for comprehensive training for all involved in this process.

On rare occasions it may be necessary for an HR professional to act in a coordinating role to assist the coach in the conduct of a formal review. This may include maintaining the integrity of the process and building competence and confidence in its application. For this to occur, the HR person must participate in the training and be competent and confident in acting as a coach.

We stress, however, that HR should not be involved in the process of performance review at all, other than to provide advice and assist line managers with any difficulties.

B: CONDUCTING A FORMAL REVIEW

Irrespective of whether the coach is conducting a benchmark review (pilot or trial) or the first formal review, it is important the review follows a carefully structured plan. For the purposes of explaining the structure, we will call it the 'feedback session'. The structure consists of six steps:

1. Planning the feedback session.

2. Preparing emotionally for the feedback session.

3. Conducting the feedback session.

4. Reaching an agreed outcome.

5. Recording the outcomes of the feedback session and planning continuous improvement/development activities.

6. Monitoring and evaluating the continuous improvement/development activities.

Step 1. Planning the feedback session

What follows in the next steps is really common sense; however, we all know what it is like to work with a manager who is weak on planning. In our training of coaches, we provide hard copy tools for ensuring a quality approach is adhered to. Here we give an overview of the critical steps that should form part of planning:

▌ Organize an environment that has sufficient space, is comfortable and interruption-free.

▌ Confirm and organize the attendance of all involved:

 - date;
 - time;
 - location.

▌ Confirm who is going to be there and what their role is to be – agree who will do the recording of discussion and outcomes.

▌ Pay serious attention to seating arrangements. Circles are less confrontational and friendlier than rectangular seating arrangements. It is worth remembering, a coach may require a one-up manager or HR person for the provision of feedback, and the employee, a union delegate for support. Two soon turns to four, which becomes a crowd.

| It is important therefore that there is a strategy to communicate with any employee representatives and/or unions. It might be necessary to involve them in the training and convince them that this process is both fair and essential to the organization's well-being. Ideally they won't need to be present at the session but if they are, you need to have a plan for dealing with them.[2] Remember, the greater the level of suspicion, the more likely a dog fight. The feedback environment must be non- threatening.

| Confirm with the employee if, besides his or her own completed feedback package, there is anything else that needs to be brought.

| Review the feedback again. Remember, it is critical to:

- focus on the job not the personality;
- focus first on success;
- clearly identify areas for improvement;
- ensure there are no surprises.

Now the coach is ready to get his or her hands dirty!

Step 2. Preparing emotionally for the feedback session

This is the point reached after all consultation has been completed with other relevant line managers and the total formal review package has been completed for each team member. All rating scales must be marked and the comments section fully completed with:

| examples of evidence – excellence and underperformance;

| notes for reinforcing expectations;

| points for discussion and agreement as to how underperformance can be dealt with;

| preliminary plan for performance improvement/individual development.

A reminder: there should be no surprises in relation to evidence in any of the listed areas of expectation. If there is any new evidence that has not been discussed previously, the coach must introduce it but not rate it formally. All evidence must be documented clearly and completed with total confidence.

Preparing emotionally is thinking through the feedback to be given to each team member and making some early judgements about how the feedback is to be given and what the likely reaction will be:

▌ How will it impact on the employee?

▌ How will the employee react?

▌ How will you, the coach, react?

▌ How might a union representative react?

▌ How will anyone else present react?

If little attention has been given to the evidence in terms of validity, reliability and consistency and it is short on examples, the review is almost guaranteed to turn into a dog fight. 'Prepare or perish' is the message.

We have discussed the importance of transparency in the performance feedback process. Notwithstanding the level of communication and consultation, both employees and coaches will be apprehensive and nervous. So too will any representatives. A coach must plan carefully what he or she will say in the first few minutes. When training coaches in the presentation of feedback, we spend a great deal of time on specially designed role plays and scenarios that deal with a broad spectrum of likely reactions and behaviours. These role plays and scenarios are purpose-designed for each organization and reflect the culture and typical contents.

In summary, preparing emotionally for the feedback session is about profiling each employee involved in formal feedback and assessing likely reactions, and making a preliminary assessment of their individual emotional state on arrival. Dealing with underperformance is a challenge – a good reason to kick off the session with most of the positive feedback you have to offer!

It is worth remembering that the employee, and if applicable the union delegate, will be doing the same thing. In particular, they will be clearly determining the coach's perceived or demonstrated strengths and weaknesses. A word of warning: if there is evidence of underperformance in your own performance, you need to be prepared for how you will deal with it.

It is also important that this aspect of preparation does not take place just prior to the session. We argue quality time should be spent in the days leading up to the formal feedback sessions.

Step 3. Conducting the feedback session

Our approach to running the session throws up the following suggestions:

- Ensure there are no interruptions and do not commence until all participants arrive, preferably together, and do not keep them waiting.

- Speak professionally but in line with the language of the workplace (within reason).

- Put everyone at ease; explain the format of the feedback session and confirm everyone is ready to commence – make eye-contact with everyone.

- Focus on excellent performance first – gain acceptance by the employee. Do not patronize.

- Focus next, and gain acceptance by the employee, on underperformance:

  - focus on evidence – provide examples when required;
  - give the employee an opportunity to respond – encourage him or her.

- Commit the employee to do more of this, or less of that.

- Target any employee concerns or assistance required.

- Make it clear to all that you are trying to help the employee, for example through the provision of additional training/development.

- Gain employee commitment to improve.

- Encourage feedback from the employee about your performance. Have a structure for this, similar to the one you use with them. 'What should I do more of/less of?' 'Please approach me on the floor if I am hindering you or I can do something to help you achieve.'

Remember, it is during this time your attention to detail in collecting evidence and completing the rating scales will win the day. There must be no doubt in your mind and you must be totally sure of what you have said and heard whilst conducting the review. Part of your planning should have determined what recording was to be done and by whom during the feedback session.

Training provided to coaches must focus on the acquisition and application of both competence and confidence. Once again, our approach is hands-on – using case studies and scenarios that escalate from a commencement point with built-in hand grenades thrown in to expose the coach to a wide range of difficult situations. This includes aggressive behaviour from the employee and even higher levels of aggression from the employee's representative. It also includes scenarios involving the HR person and the difficult role he or she sometimes has. This allows all participants in the training to see various ways of dealing with poor conduct. Those who play the roles must adopt the behaviours of someone who intends winning at all costs.

In conducting the formal review, the coach must be prepared to deliver a strong disciplinary message from time to time. It may be that the coach ultimately has to tell the employee in the strongest possible terms that he or she has not performed to standard and this is what he or she has to do about it – 'You must lift your game by doing/not doing the following' – be specific!

Chapter 7 will deal with how the coach moves from a coaching role to a disciplinary role as a prelude to the road to goodbye.

Finally, as in the case of any situation where evidence is presented and discussed, there comes a point where a verdict has to be reached. The verdict in a formal review is where the coach has presented the individual evidence and the employee and coach have agreed to:

- the ratings on each of the areas of expectations;
- what is excellent performance;
- what is underperformance;
- what specifically needs to be improved/developed.

Step 4. Reaching an agreed outcome

Reaching agreed outcomes is a critical step in the performance feedback process (closing the deal). It is the culmination of all the hard work in:

- collecting the evidence and examples;
- planning the feedback session;
- preparing emotionally;
- conducting the feedback session.

There is a skill in reaching agreement. Any salesperson will talk of the importance of closing a deal. The acquisition and application of this skill must be part of the training provided to coaches.

We believe a telling way to illustrate this process is through the things a hard-nosed coach in the world of underground mining did to ensure he was able to reach an agreed outcome with each of the employees in his team. The words are as he stated them, and can be amended to suit any work environment:

I Really know your people.

I Tell people the truth, not bullshit – it must be the way it is.

I Plan carefully what you will say and how you will say it. People will be apprehensive, tense and nervous.

I Take time to put people at ease.

I People can be surprised at how you rate them. Your ratings may not match their own.

I Your first rating of people will turn out to be close to the mark.

I Evidence used must be accurate.

I Never change your ratings during an interview (pass on it and come back to them).

I Unless you have all the evidence, don't argue a point – come back on another day.

I You must know and articulate clearly to an employee what is required (expectations) in order to improve performance.

I Set and stick to improvement/development plans.

I The employee must be encouraged to provide feedback to the team leader about what he or she should or could do to assist the employee improve/maintain/develop his or her performance and agree to act on it.

Once the outcome has been agreed to, the coach and employee can jointly map out an improvement/development plan.

Step 5. Recording the outcomes of the feedback session and planning continuous improvement/development activities

This stage is about confirming joint agreement in areas to be improved and how it will be done. The focus is then on a coaching plan that addresses the area(s) that must be improved. It might also be development as part of preparing for future changes in work responsibilities.

One area agreed for improvement might be behaviour (code of conduct), for example, absenteeism or punctuality. It may include housekeeping or the use of personal protective equipment. For a teacher it might be the return of assignments in a timely manner and a greater level of written feedback. This coaching plan is not too involved, rather an agreement to change behaviour. This agreement must be monitored by the coach.

On the other hand, an area for improvement might relate to competence to do the job; the inability to meet a standard, which ultimately means training is required. Where this occurs, the coach will need to prepare a coaching plan that focuses on training and further development. This coaching plan might involve all team members. It may be characteristic of all team members.

The training and development might emerge from an increase in rework, the inability to troubleshoot, or may relate to new equipment. It might also relate to operating a computer for maximum potential or developing and presenting proposals/reports.[3] It might be to deal with student complaints or class/subject dropouts.

This coaching plan requires a clear specification for learning and assessment and is completed over time. This is a more formal agreement, which must be monitored by the coach.[4]

Whatever the focus of the coaching plan, there must be agreement on what needs to be improved, how it will be improved, and an agreement by the coach and the employee to meet at a set time in the future to review progress and confirm compliance.

Planning continuous improvement activities should:

▌ set clear objectives;

▌ establish and agree on priorities;

▌ set and agree on timelines;

▌ target the coaching assistance required and how learning will occur:

- mentoring,
- formal training,
- work shadowing (spending time with a top performer),
- job rotation,
- exchanges,
- projects;

▌ target resources required;

▌ complete individual and team coaching (development) plan;

▌ set a date for the next formal feedback session;

▌ sign off on the coaching plan.

Coaching plans must be specific and clearly note:

- areas for improvement;
- action to be taken;
- resources to be committed;
- date to be commenced;
- date for completion or review.

They must be signed off by all involved.

All coaching plans should be accompanied by a clearly set out timetable for future reviews. In the case of a benchmark review, it should be accompanied by follow-up reviews.

It must be stressed that this stage underpins the integrity of the entire formal feedback process. It is where the coach and the organization demonstrate their commitment to the continuous improvement/development of all employees. It should be very easy for a coach to tell someone they have performed excellently. It is another matter when time and resources have to be committed to addressing underperformance. This is where the commitment is tested. A lot of organizations are not great at maintaining the momentum and seeing things through to the end.

The coach has one more critical step to pursue.

Step 6. Monitoring and evaluating the continuous improvement/development activities

Action, we are told, speaks louder than words. Words written on a coaching plan might read and sound good, but without action they are meaningless. Often the coach may have to hand over coaching/development plans to someone else, such as a training department. The coach must 'ride shotgun' in these instances.

Where behaviour is involved, it means following up commitments to improve. Where competence is involved, it may mean using a skilled operator to assist in learning and ultimately assessment.

This stage requires the coach to:

- ensure the coaching/improvement/development plan is implemented;
- check on progress in meeting objectives and timelines;
- target and deal with any difficulties in achieving the coaching plan;

- provide support and encouragement;

- continue informal on the job (in the workplace) feedback and coaching;

- organize and conduct formal off the job (outside the workplace) feedback and coaching.

This stage requires continuous vigilance of both normal work activities and development activities. It must be part of the everyday coaching role of the line manager.

In addition, the coach will need to provide concrete examples of improvement in job performance to senior managers. This might be through:

- reduction in lost time injuries;

- reduction in rework;

- reduction in absenteeism;

- improved morale;

- improved throughput of product;

- reduction in customer complaints, or return of product;

- reduction in student complaints/withdrawals.

As stated earlier, the line manager's performance improvement/development plan will be inclusive of all of the activities contained in the individual coaching plans. Some of these can have monetary values put on them over time; greater attention will be given to this in Chapter 8.

A final but important point needs to be made as we conclude this chapter. Where the coaching plan relates to unacceptable conduct, the price of continued non-compliance must be communicated to the employee at every stage of coaching – 'If this behaviour continues you could lose your job.' This is the message they have to hear.

Taking stock again

In the last three chapters covering workplace coaching, we have moved through a series of stages:

- Setting the scene for workplace coaching.

- Getting the right people on your team.

- What is workplace coaching?

I Workplace coaching in action.

I Operating on the job (during work activities).

I Operating off the job (during a formal review).

I Designing a structure for a formal review.

I Marking a rating scale.

I Conducting a formal review off the job.

We do not believe all line managers have the kitbag of competences required to engage in workplace coaching as part of managing people. The next chapter deals with our learning approach to preparing line managers to do this competently and confidently.

NOTES

1. Theoretically this should not happen. If the attendance policy requires certain things they should be built in to the day-to-day feedback – the employee should have been challenged on his or her return from the absence.

2. Unions and employee representatives should be advised that there is a process for dealing with grievances if anything untoward is said to have occurred in the process.

3. The culmination of the individual/team coaching plans should take the line manager to the point where he or she can develop a performance improvement plan for their area for submission to their manager.

4. For higher level managers who have predetermined Key Performance Indicators (KPIs) and Key Result Areas (KRAs) in respect to their area of management, the performance improvement plan will highlight the actions to be taken by the manager to achieve the turnaround in performance needed.

6

Developing coaches for managing people

In Chapters 3, 4 and 5 we introduced you to the cornerstone of our approach to managing people – workplace coaching. Central to our discussions was the changed nature of workplace relationships, the importance of the coach being involved in getting the right people on the team, the activities involved in workplace coaching, and the principles that should be in place to ensure success.

Our discussions extended to the kitbag of competences required for a coach to operate effectively on the job on a day-to-day basis through the provision of informal feedback, and off the job through the provision of feedback during a formal review. To operate as a coach on a day-to-day basis requires both competence and confidence in the normal management role, and extending these to include the ongoing development of each employee, and when it is obvious coaching is not working, the necessary disciplinary action. Chapter 7 deals with this.

We begin with some observations:

We do not believe that line managers have the kitbag of competences and behaviour required to engage in workplace coaching as part of a comprehensive approach to managing people.

▌ Many organizations approach the preparation/development of workplace coaches through training based on what senior managers think will be good for them.

▌ Far too many training programmes are taken off the shelf; worse, are based on bite-sized learning rather than a holistic approach.

▌ Many organizations do not apply the process described for getting the right people on the team.

▌ Learning (or training in this case) must be directly related to the expectations (performance and behaviour) the coach is required to demonstrate as part of the organization's purpose-designed approach to managing people. Learning must therefore focus on the development of a unique set of competences that allow this to happen.

Senior managers want results. However, as far as providing learning opportunities that genuinely respond to employee learning needs and deliver real development, they often do not do what they need to do to get it right. The individual and team development plans that fall out of the formal review process and reflect, in part, day-to-day feedback, necessitate genuine responses to learning needs. The same process must apply to the learning provided to those line managers who will act as workplace coaches and are responsible for the development and maintenance of these plans.

In summary, the development of competent and confident workplace coaches is one of the critical success factors in managing people. To assist you in taking charge of the developmental process, we have structured this chapter in two parts: A, Learning design, and B, Training design.

All involved need to recognize and deal with the reality that quite a few things will change as a result of this approach. Line managers will see themselves and colleagues behaving in appropriate and inappropriate ways. Each will be asked to change the way they behave. They will receive direct, hard-hitting feedback that will build solidarity in the way people are managed.

Part A, Learning design, focuses on how we manage learning. It consists of our approach and incorporates the activities that drive learning and how we assess (make judgements) on the extent to which learning is successful. Part B, Training design, focuses on how we facilitate learning so that we make sure it is successful and achieves what we have forecast it should achieve (outcomes).

In summary, Part A is about the learning process. It is about designing activities that allow the acquired competence and confidence to be transferred from an artificial workplace environment to the unscripted world of work. Part B is about how we as trainers and purveyors of learning engage in complementary activities that drive the learning process. This is where we adopt the role of learning facilitators and collaborators. It is of little consequence what you call yourself when involved in these activities; it is what you do that matters. However, more of that in Part B. For now we turn to Part A, Learning design.

A: LEARNING DESIGN

Designing learning so it is right

The world of work has become overrun by people flogging the competency-based movement. What should be simple has, for many organizations, become cumbersome, arduous and expensive. This is not a book about theories of learning. However, we will describe our approach in broad terms, which ensures that when we engage line managers in learning how to become effective workplace coaches, we follow a tried and true strategy.

We use a performance-based and criterion-referenced approach to learning. 'Performance-based' means the competences and behaviour required of a coach must ultimately be demonstrated on the job under operational conditions without supervision. 'Criterion-referenced' means the nature of the performance, the conditions under which or with what the performance will take place, and the standard of performance required, must be clearly specified and replicate the world of work.

Performance-based learning requires assessment of performance (feedback on performance through learning). Once we know the performance required of workplace coaches, we design the assessment process. When you change the way you assess people, you change the way you teach people. You change the way people learn. This is critical – learning by doing, not through telling and listening, although sometimes this will occur.

This simply means our assessment process involves demonstrating competence and behaviour in real-life simulations, leading to actually doing it on the job, initially with a support person. Assessment design up front has a major impact on how learning will occur and how it must involve practice, periods of consolidation and constant application. We recreate life in the organization and acknowledge it is based on the goodies and baddies who live in it. There is no point creating a pure, clinical environment just because one of the senior managers is religious and doesn't swear. The learning environment is mediated by the culture and behaviour that exist. We do, of course, work to change this in order to build respect, truth and honest relationships as part of learning.

Formal assessment ultimately takes place when the learner is confident to perform on his or her own. This is also where support personnel expand their role to include formal assessment as required. Depending on the size of the organization, this may become a major consideration in learning design (we still have to run a business). In assessment terms, it is not just about suitability and cost-effectiveness, but results.

At the end of the day unless someone can perform on the job under operational conditions without supervision, they cannot be deemed competent or confident, so their likely performance on the job is questionable. We also acknowledge there are lots of confident incompetent people around who fall into categories of:

- unconsciously incompetent;

- consciously incompetent;

- consciously competent;

- unconsciously competent.

In summary, the design of learning for workplace coaches requires:

- a clear specification of the performance required on the job, day-to-day;

- a clear identification of what needs to be learnt to match the performance required;

- an assessment strategy to assess the performance required;

- a clear plan of how learning will be acquired and applied;

- a clear plan of the resources and support necessary, and how these will be managed to ensure sustainable and confident performance over time.

We need workplace coaches who have the competence, behaviour and confidence to operate with their team, on and off the job, with the support of skilled facilitators of learning, acting as mentors/coaches in the workplace during the development process. The design of learning should be simple and clearly structured. We provide a structure consisting of five steps to ensure success, summarized in Figure 6.1.

To date we have not been prescriptive about what coaches need to learn. This may vary within organizations. But we have, in Chapters 4 and 5, provided a clear guide by describing what is involved.

We now turn to what we call a 'building-block approach' to the development of workplace coaches. We translate what we have said thus far in this

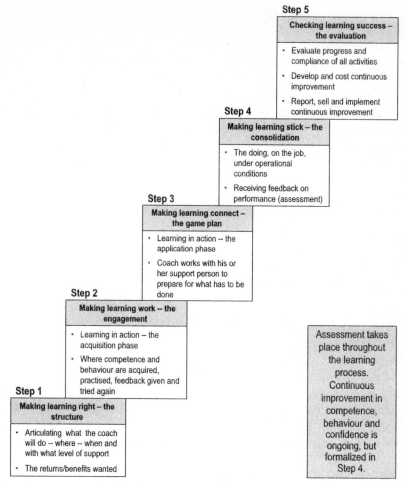

Step 5

Checking learning success – the evaluation

- Evaluate progress and compliance of all activities
- Develop and cost continuous improvement
- Report, sell and implement continuous improvement

Step 4

Making learning stick – the consolidation

- The doing, on the job, under operational conditions
- Receiving feedback on performance (assessment)

Step 3

Making learning connect – the game plan

- Learning in action -- the application phase
- Coach works with his or her support person to prepare for what has to be done

Step 2

Making learning work -- the engagement

- Learning in action -- the acquisition phase
- Where competence and behaviour are acquired, practised, feedback given and tried again

Step 1

Making learning right – the structure

- Articulating what the coach will do -- where -- when and with what level of support
- The returns/benefits wanted

Assessment takes place throughout the learning process. Continuous improvement in competence, behaviour and confidence is ongoing, but formalized in Step 4.

Figure 6.1   Five steps to managing sustainable learning

chapter into five steps for sustainable learning, describing what must take place at each step. We call these five steps the 'management of learning'.

Before we commence our walk up the steps to sustainable learning, another suggestion. Our approach will require the coaches to learn in different ways. This means hard work. Some will complain about how hard it is. Senior managers will need to be clear and supportive of the learning process. Learning, which is purpose- designed to assist coaches to do their jobs better, requires a 'can do' mentality.

To reach this state of mind, the learning process must be transparent and provide the right mix of know, do, think and conform to (comply with). It must also be designed so coaches are able to transfer their learning to current and new situations. Diagnosis, problem solving and troubleshooting must be integrated into the learning process.

Five steps to managing sustainable (lasting) learning

Figure 6.1 consists of five building blocks. These building blocks represent a sequence of critical activities that must occur to ensure that the learning provided to coaches is relevant, interactive, sustainable, and works. The five building blocks are steps:

1. Making learning right – the structure.

2. Making learning work – the engagement.

3. Making learning connect – the game plan.

4. Making learning stick – the consolidation.

5. Checking learning success – the evaluation.

Each building block has a clear statement of performance, for example: Step 1. Making learning right – the structure, and a brief description of what needs to occur.

Step 1. Making learning right – the structure

If we want capable and confident workplace coaches, the organization, through its senior managers, must be totally clear about what they want them to do and the level of commitment and support to be provided. There must be total consistency – clarity of what people management means to the organization, the principles to be applied, and the practice required of line managers when acting in their role of workplace coach. This commitment must extend to the need for consistent vigilance and action over excellence and underperformance.

There must be total consistency in how areas of performance improvement/development will be dealt with. All managers and coaches must 'sing from the same hymn book', and all employees must know what hymn is being sung and the key it is being sung in.

Step 1 also represents what all the employees in the organization need to know about managing people, its principles and practice, and how it can be made simple. Members of the shop floor team – the recipients of coaching – will need to know how it will operate and the returns/benefits that will flow, in particular the consequences if they do not respond to the feedback and plans to improve their individual performance as required. (See more in Chapter 7.)

Step 2. Making learning work – the engagement

This step is where the coach begins the interactive learning process, where competence, behaviour and confidence (capability) are acquired. It is where purpose- designed learning activities allow the coach to see and experience underperformance, inappropriate behaviour and a lack of confidence when dealing with an employee. It also allows each coach to witness the reverse: exemplary approaches to dealing with an employee who is either underperforming or performing excellently.

There is an opportunity to make a first-hand assessment of what not to do and make judgements about how to do it. It provides a powerful tool for retentive learning. Each coach is involved (as are the learning facilitators) in the interactive learning activities by getting their hands dirty and is provided with objective feedback, particularly from peers, as well as the facilitators. The focus is on continuous improvement and opportunities for further practice and consolidation, and the development of a can-do mentality.

In designing learning activities, it is important not to create a circus. Learning should not be totally activities-based. There must be some down-to-earth knowledge building through formal presentations, and higher level thinking through questioning, scenarios and case studies. It is a 'horses for courses' approach.

Our recommendation is that case studies or scenarios, using fishbowls and triads, are the best way to acquire and apply competence, confidence and behaviour for this learning need. These allow the coach to experience the feeling of getting it wrong and getting it right; to receive feedback and suggestions for improvement; to practise again in an atmosphere of assault, support and continuous improvement, but flavoured with a pinch of discipline as required.

Case studies and scenarios must be organization-based, using real-life workplace examples, but avoiding personalities. Each must be carefully scripted to meet the specific learning outcome sought. It is the fishbowl approach (gazing in from outside) which brings each learning situation alive. It simply means being able to see them in action and detect what is going on, make judgements about what is seen and, more important, how to do it better by rectifying one's behaviour.

Step 2 is where the essential capabilities for a coach to engage employees, whilst operating both on and off the job, are acquired. The coach learns to:

▌ provide performance feedback;

▌ engage employees in the workplace;

▌ manage underperformance;

gather evidence;

prepare for a formal review;

conduct a formal review.

This learning is designed to be interactive. Examples of how learning is made interactive are provided below.

Fishbowls

Remember these must be organization-based, not taken out of a book. They must be carefully scripted and totally focused on the knowledge, skills (practical and low and high level thinking) and attitudes to be acquired and later applied. Some would argue these have to be sanitized. We say no. They must replicate what goes on in the workplace. This is particularly important because, in the case of a code of conduct, it represents the behaviours we are seeking to change. We make the point here that fishbowls and triads coexist as part of learning.

We use fishbowls to deal with competence, either unacceptable or excellent performance. It involves the coaches in learning and might require one to play the role of an employee who is working on the job, and is approached by a coach who has detected non-compliance to a standard of performance. It may be a breach in safety, incorrect use of a piece of equipment, or incorrect posture at a computer. It might be an unacceptable level of untidiness or incorrectly dealing with a customer or student/fellow teacher (building blocks 1 and 2). This is where the GIDAY strategy comes alive. The coach and the employee act their individual, tightly-scripted role, under the observation of the learning facilitators and other coaches in training.

It is imperative that a thorough debrief occurs and the performance of the coach is put under the microscope. This process creates great opportunities for learning. Often skills that can never be read about in books are demonstrated by the coach. (Many coaches who see themselves as poor communicators are often the stars. Never underestimate the capability of any line manager.) Coaches learn other ways of doing. Additionally, some coaches, unhappy with their performance, want to try again using the feedback they have received.

We also use fishbowls to deal with conduct. For example it might be unacceptable levels of absenteeism, or unacceptable behaviour as a team member.

The success of fishbowls based on purpose-written case studies or scenarnarios cannot be overstated. Their greater value is when each is extended to include changing circumstances. For example, a coach approaches an employee who is continually late. Using the GIDAY strategy, he receives an undertaking from the employee that he or she will improve. Alas, two weeks later the employee is back to unacceptable behaviour.

The use of the original case study/scenario to expand into more serious examples of unacceptable performance and conduct allows for the introduction and development of skills in dealing with conflict, negotiation, counselling and discipline.

Triads

This is a first class strategy for allowing coaches to get their minds tuned into conducting a formal review and feedback session in a workshop environment. Each coach prepares for their first formal review by selecting a member of their team who has a mixture of excellent and underperformance.

Evidence is gathered and documentation is completed, based on facts about the team member in key expectations. This is finalized and time spent on preparing for the review. In doing so, each coach uses the tools developed to help the review in being conducted reliably and professionally.

Coaches are divided into groups of two and are allocated a support person who will observe each coach in turn conducting their review (hence the term 'triad'). The second coach plays the role of the employee and reacts to the feedback given. There is no specific script, but the second coach uses the competence and behaviour acquired during the learning to react accordingly. For example, the evidence might be suspect without actual examples; there may be surprises, evidence may not have included one-up manager feedback. It becomes the role of the coach to sell the integrity, validity and fairness of the review. The role of the other coach, as employee, is to challenge realistically what is presented.

By the completion of Step 2, those coaches who are likely to struggle have been identified. An individual development plan designed to provide specific assistance on an ongoing basis has been prepared and discussed with the coach and their support person.

Step 3. Making learning connect – the game plan

This is where the quality and integrity of learning are put to the test. It is where a substantial portion of the learning is applied. The coach now returns to the workplace to prepare for a formal review. It is where much of the competence and behaviour acquired now finds its home.

Step 3 is where coaches learn how to:

- gather evidence;
- complete the documentation;
- plan the process;
- rehearse the process.

The gathering of evidence does not present any great difficulty. In fact, most coaches realize how critical evidence of performance is in the formal feedback process and spend a lot of time consulting with one-up managers and getting it right.

Completing the documentation rarely presents a problem. Because the evidence gathering has been so focused, the subsequent completion of rating scales is clear and precise. However, it is important that the rating scale is clear, specific and easy to complete. (See examples in Chapter 5.)

Planning the process, and rehearsing the process, is often where the 'butterflies' begin to emerge. Butterflies are directly related to the known behaviour of individual team members and perceptions of likely individual reactions.[1] At this point the support person needs to be tuned into the level of support required. Each coach in training is provided with quality control sheets that set out the process of planning and conducting a review; however most still need support aimed at further confidence building.

This is an important time in the learning process for coaches and the implementation of people management. This is where the commitment of senior managers in the organization, to supply the resources and support, is put to the test. Without continued support the entire learning process is put at risk.

We now move to a critical phase. This is where we want those competences and behaviour learnt and practised by the coach to stick. Learning cannot be said to have stuck unless it is applied consistently on the job. There is a need for day-to-day, week-to-week use. When the design of learning is correct, sticking means continual use. (It is the transfer of learning from the training room to the real world of the unscripted workplace. This is the challenge of any learning/training.) It is an extension of relevant learning – learning that is right for the needs of the coach whilst managing the performance of the team.

Step 4. Making learning stick – the consolidation

This step is where the main game occurs. All the learning, practice and preparation are applied to the conduct of a formal feedback session with an employee. At this point of learning the coach is conducting a benchmark review (see page 63) where no final judgements are made on new evidence introduced at that time. Any new evidence that has not been discussed with an employee in the workplace (GIDAY) has been gathered during Step 3.

This is also where excellent performance is acknowledged. Our experience has been that many excellent performers are often unaware of their level of performance because feedback in most organizations is only given when an employee messes up, or because their positive contributions are far too often ignored or feedback is seen as unnecessary amidst a busy work schedule.

Following a final double-check of what is required, the coach then commences the formal review by focusing and reaching agreement on:

I where the employee is now;

I where the employee should be in six months;

I what plan is needed to improve/develop the employee;

I implementing an improvement/development plan;

I monitoring the improvement plan in the workplace – is it happening?

The focus on improvement covers those areas described in Steps 1 to 5 on pages 87–94. The importance and benefit of the benchmark review as part of the learning application is that it makes allowance for the coach making some minor errors. Ultimately, it is about the coach and the employee reaching agreement on the performance and conduct indicators.

During the learning consolidation process the coach is using purpose-designed quality control sheets. They guide the coach to deal with excellent performance first, then move into areas for improvement, reaching agreement on areas for improvement/development, and completing a plan that details what will happen from here on.

Finally, the coach evaluates the progress of the plan. The coach:

I ensures the plan is implemented;

I checks on the employee's progress;

I targets any difficulties;

I provides support, encouragement and feedback;

I organizes and conducts the next formal feedback session;

I continues the coaching process on the job.

These activities require the coach to increase his or her visibility on the job. It is imperative a coach does not spend his or her time warming an office seat at the expense of being constantly seen. Such behaviour is always a reliable indicator of pending trouble at any time in our approach to managing people.

We conclude this step with an emphasis on another aspect of learning that receives close attention during Step 2, Learning – the engagement. In some organizations, employees may want to bring a union official when they turn up for their benchmark review. Chances are the review will turn into a dog fight if the union official and employee have preconceived views on the validity and reliability of the evidence or the motives of senior management. Union officials will turn up if the entire people management process has been badly communicated or poorly sold to employees, or lacks total commitment from the top. This can often be viewed as organized labour using adversarial tactics to discipline poor management.

Step 5. Checking learning success – the evaluation

This step is about getting feedback on the extent to which the organization's investment is having the desired impact. This is not a book about evaluation, but it is about obtaining evidence if:

▌ coaches are operating effectively both on and off the job (effectiveness relating to the detection of underperformance);

▌ support people are providing the level of support required and this support is having a real impact on the work of coaches;

▌ improvement/development plans are meeting individual and team learning needs and are having a direct impact on improving the way work is done;

▌ the cost of improvement is being related to real financial gains in the workplace, for example:

- improved safety performance (reduction in lost time injuries),
- reduction in rework,
- improved equipment reliability,
- reduction in absenteeism/truancy,
- reduction in customer returns,
- improved team/workplace morale,
- reduction in customer/student complaints.

Some of these will be able to have a financial value put on them; others will be nebulous but important, such as improved customer satisfaction. (This will be dealt with further in Chapter 8.)

Reporting on progress and improvement should become a good news story. All employees have been involved in the development of the people management system. It becomes a critical task to report to them on its impact and success.

There is always room for improvement. If the people management process is supported, the workforce will want to know how it is progressing and play a role in its improvement. Ultimately, it is about seeking continuous improvement in how people management is done.

Summary

Developing workplace coaches to operate and behave to a standard is a challenging task. To do it correctly, the organization, through its managers, employees and union delegates, must be totally clear and agreed on what competences and behaviour a coach must possess and how these will be acquired and applied to ensure success.

It must be acknowledged upfront that some line managers are likely to be poor performers. Our experience has been that these people fall by the wayside before or during the learning process. When this occurs, we argue it becomes nearly impossible to retain such a person as a line manager responsible for the performance of a team under their control.

Just as some employees will be underperformers, there will be underperforming coaches. In both instances, there may come a time when all help to improve has failed; when those managers responsible must move from coaching mode to discipline mode. We deal with this in the next chapter.

We conclude with a reminder. Should you want to implement a tried, proven and can-do approach to the development of your workplace coaches, remember, there is no substitute for a purpose-designed programme to fit your own organization.

We have consulted in organizations whose senior managers have wanted to take training programmes off the shelf or who want to provide small, bite-sized pieces of learning over time, for example, this month 'Negotiation', in two months 'Conflict Resolution'. It does not work if sustainable (lasting) results are required because it does not support a purpose-built people management system.

Another word of caution. Be careful who you select to conduct the training. We have seen academics make the journey from the classroom to a coal mine for the first time and, when confronted with employee resistance, they turn to water. This is not to say this is the norm. Nor is it to say a hard-nosed consultant will succeed when moving from the coal mine to a group of priests or nuns. Adjustments to style and language are always required.

In Part B which follows, we turn to training design. It is an overview of how we facilitate the learning process based on the culture of the organization (the way things are done), where the organization is currently, where it needs to be taken to and how the people management system will work. Our training design is a complementary process to learning design. It allows us to work and control learning for maximum benefit.

B: TRAINING DESIGN

Designing training so it is right

Part A of this chapter provided an overview of the learning process based on five steps to manage learning that lasts. Particular emphasis was placed on the design of assessment and how, when you change the way you assess and the way you teach, you change the way people learn. This is a major consideration for any training or learning facilitator.

Equal emphasis was placed on the importance of designing learning to be interactive. Examples of fishbowls and triads were provided to reinforce how learning must involve practice and consolidation. Part B gives a description of how we, as trainers (learning directors, facilitators and collaborators, used interchangeably) work and control the learning process.

We do this by breaking down each of the five steps to manage sustainable learning (see Figure 6.1, page 87) into each of their own individual steps or building blocks. This allows for a clearer delineation of what it is we do when working and controlling the learning process. It is important to note that the last building block in each of the major steps shows the connection to the next major step.

We begin with a word of caution. Learning design does not begin where the learning process begins, in the artificial environment of a training room. Anyone seeking to develop workplace coaches must begin by being involved in gaining the organization's commitment to the approach to be used in managing people. This also requires being involved during the process of identifying and developing key result areas.

Critical point of linking learning design and training design

We issue another caution. You may find some repetition in what follows, but we believe this to be an advantage because the sub-steps actually specify what has to be done and draw together key elements of previous chapters. For example, you may say to yourself as you read, what is being described is in fact learning. It is really about being more specific about the role of the trainer in driving learning, taking control and working the process with authority. There is always a great challenge in the design of learning, exceeded only by the challenge to the trainer to be totally professional in the management of learning.

Irrespective of whether you are an external consultant or an internal consultant/employee, you must drive the process confidently, with a clearly articulated plan of activities. If you do not, you will more than likely fail. There is too much at stake for this to happen.

The explanation that follows provides footprints to a clearly constructed plan. Much of it is self-explanatory. When you link Parts A and B of this chapter you should be able to successfully develop coaches for their important role of managing people. Whilst a plan is critical, you still have to manage the learners during a very difficult change process.

To assist you to follow the footprints, examine the chart shown in Figure 6.2 as part of your preparation.[2] The chart is simple, but we must always be very clear about the role of each of these key players involved in learning. This allows the trainer(s) to ensure an uninterrupted process and target any non-compliance which ultimately may impact on the quality of learning.

Training design specified outcomes	BEFORE Preparation	DURING Off the job	AFTER On the job
Role of trainer			
Role of trainees			
Role of workplace management			

Figure 6.2 Training transfer model

You will notice the boxes under 'Before', 'During' and 'After' are empty. We invite you to fill in the boxes when you have finished reading this chapter. It will help you clarify key indicators for success.

Step 1. Making learning right – the structure

This step consists of five sub-steps or building blocks; see Figure 6.3. The five steps provide an overview of what is involved. It provides the trainers, trainees and management a clear direction via the footprints that are to be followed. More importantly, it provides the trainer(s) with milestones that have to be achieved on the road to learning. No step begins unless the trainers have accomplished and gained agreement on what is required. For example, the two larger boxes attached to sub-steps 4 and 5 are the lynchpins of step 1. If the contents set out in these boxes have not been scrutinized and agreed to by those being trained as coaches, success is less likely.

Another important thing to reaffirm at this point is that what is contained in each of the five sub-steps summarizes what we have discussed in Chapters 1 to 5. The contents should serve as a quality control check. It should allow for the identification of any critical success factor that may have been overlooked. We encourage you to pause and imagine you are driving your organization's approach to managing people. Irrespective of whether you are running the training you should now be in a position of clarity and confidence as to how to proceed.

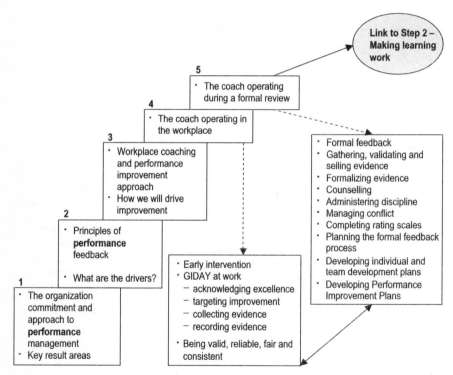

Figure 6.3   Step 1 – Making learning right – the structure

Step 2. Making learning work – the engagement

Step 2 is where learning begins. Figure 6.4 consists of six sub-steps and identifies six of the key learning activities described in Part A of this chapter. Trainees are involved in learning acquisition (off the job) in a workshop

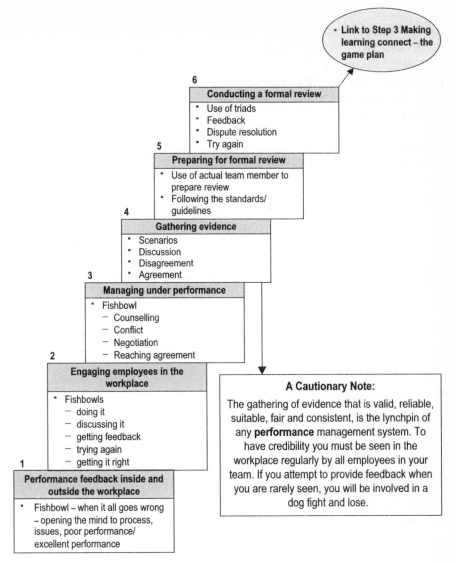

Figure 6.4 Step 2 – Making learning work – the engagement

setting. It also requires preparation for learning application on the job (in the real world where work takes place).

These learning activities must be skilfully managed by the trainer(s). There is no room for subjectivity. Connections between knowing and doing must be tightly controlled. Careful attention must be given to messages gleaned from the completed individual profile of each participant gathered prior to

commencing learning. Individual differences should be considered in preparation for providing feedback on performance.

The learning activities that occur are so real that often the personalities of
participants may change when placed in challenging situations. It is imperative that trainers are prepared for the behaviours that might emerge when
the challenges impact on individuals.

Sometimes these activities highlight individuals who should never have
been appointed as line managers. On the other hand, these activities can
reveal real success stories – coaches who just 'take off' at this point in learning.

One thing is certain. Never use trainers who are incapable of managing
mood swings with either individuals or groups. Any trainer must be able to
think quickly when responding to changes in individual and group behaviours, particularly during uncertain moments and phases. One of the great
strengths of a trainer is debriefing learning activities. This skill must come to
the fore during these six sub-steps. There is nothing more frustrating for
learners than to be involved in an activity and then have it left to die without
a clear strategy for application, without reaching conclusions and messages
for professional practice.

A final word on this step. The trainer must practise what is preached about
validity, reliability and fairness when making judgements about performance
and behaviour during fishbowls and triads. Simply, there is a time to be nice
and a time to be nasty – but you had better be right, convincing and professional, and be sure you are following specified and known criteria that are
clearly communicated to all involved. There must be no surprises.

Step 3. Making learning connect – the game plan

It is important to repeat that each of the five major steps in the learning process is connected. From a learning point of view these connections continue
the footprints for success. From a trainer's point of view, Steps 3 and 4 are
the most critical. Without tight management controls, the value of learning
that occurred in Step 2 can be put at risk or even lost.

Step 3 is where the application of learning in the real world begins; see
Figure 6.5. Close scrutiny of each of the four sub-steps will show that each
coach in training is now engaged in operating as a coach on a day-to-day
basis, using the GIDAY approach during work activities and preparing to
conduct a formal review (see Chapters 3 and 4).

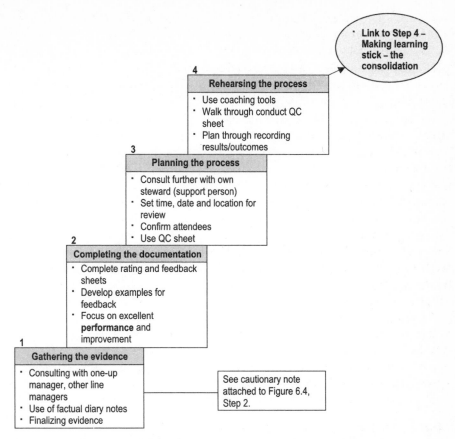

Figure 6.5   Step 3 – Making learning connect – the game plan

Continued support is of paramount importance. All of this support has been planned and committed to, set in concrete by senior managers and agreed to by all employees through the communication and consultation process (see Chapters 1 and 2). In organizations that have been successful in implementing our approach, the level of planning and commitment undertaken, promised and complied with, ensures Steps 3 and 4 survive and flourish.

From your own knowledge and experience you know that learning environments, away from the real world of work, should isolate participants from the day-to-day challenges of their job. However, the reality of returning to the job to apply learning whilst managing normal work activities provides a first class opportunity for learning to be sacrificed – 'I'll do that tomorrow'.

This step must be totally managed and facilitated by the trainers. It is where the commitment of management and the trainees is called upon. As trainers we let loose the reins of control to others to steward on the job performance; we referred to these people as 'support persons' in Part A of this chapter.

In some of the organizations where we have implemented our people management approach, these support people have been called 'mentors'. In some instances they have been HR personnel; it depends on the size and structure of the organization. Irrespective of title, what these people are required to do must be totally clear. Each must be trained and given time to do what is required. We refer to this important role and work as an 'immunization strategy' to combat failure.

Our view is that this loosening of the reins *need not* happen, but really *should.* Costs will have a major bearing. For example, if external trainers are to manage the application of learning performance on the job, it will come at high cost. If the organization's senior management decide to have their own learning facilitators/managers steward the process, it will also come at a cost, because these people will need to be given time to do what is required.

The major considerations are embedding the learning successfully into the organization and ensuring that the people responsible are able to confidently manage the entire process in a sustainable way. Confidence is a can-do ethos. The most important thing is that the forecast outcomes are achieved and produce the results that will deliver real and sustainable benefits to all. It is the very reason the organization has introduced a people management approach.

Step 4. Making learning stick – the consolidation

Step 4 consists of five sub-steps; see Figure 6.6. There is no more critical step than consolidation of learning. Whatever support/stewarding process is selected by the organization's senior management, it becomes imperative to watch over the on the job activities and the individual behaviour of each coach under the pressures of doing it in the real world of work.

The trainers and trainees have spent hours preparing for the moment. Trainees have used a great deal of energy preparing themselves. Some may have fallen by the wayside, but those who remain are committed and primed to implement workplace coaching. The coaching principles must be complied with. The evidence collected in order to give feedback during a formal review must be valid, reliable, suitable and fair. There must be no surprises. All the operating performance standards and the code of conduct specified for a coach must be complied with.

The learning activities designed and implemented in Step 2 to prepare workplace coaches will have each coach confident. However, there is nothing like doing it in an environment which actually replicates the living

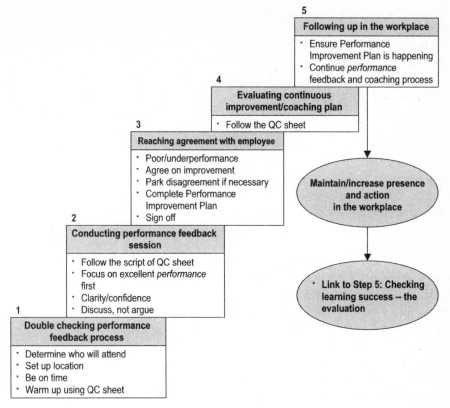

5

Following up in the workplace

- Ensure Performance Improvement Plan is happening
- Continue *performance* feedback and coaching process

4

Evaluating continuous improvement/coaching plan

- Follow the QC sheet

3

Reaching agreement with employee

- Poor/underperformance
- Agree on improvement
- Park disagreement if necessary
- Complete Performance Improvement Plan
- Sign off

Maintain/increase presence and action in the workplace

2

Conducting performance feedback session

- Follow the script of QC sheet
- Focus on excellent *performance* first
- Clarity/confidence
- Discuss, not argue

- **Link to Step 5: Checking learning success -- the evaluation**

1

Double checking performance feedback process

- Determine who will attend
- Set up location
- Be on time
- Warm up using QC sheet

Figure 6.6   Step 4 – Making learning stick – the consolidation

environment of work. The trainers have provided each coach with quality control (QC) sheets to follow whilst preparing for and conducting a formal review with an employee. These are to assist in practice and implementation; to maintain consistency/reliability with each employee; and to assist each coach to conduct the formal review with confidence.

At this point, the development of each employee and improving workplace performance are the focus of the coach. Individual development plans are finalized and implemented. The employees are involved in having their performance and behaviour reported on. Excellent performance is acknowledged and underperformance becomes the blueprint for development and improvement.

As with any work activities based on expectations (standards and a code of conduct), compliance becomes a major activity. This requires the implementation of an evaluation that targets the critical success factors involved in the people management approach. This leads to the final step, Step 5.

Step 5. Checking learning success – the evaluation

This step consists of four sub-steps; see Figure 6.7. In our experience most organizations have a reluctance to, lack of interest in, or are just ignorant of how important it is to evaluate the success of learning and training. Often any evaluation consists of 'happy sheets' that give some subjective feedback on matters to do with how well the trainees enjoyed a training programme.

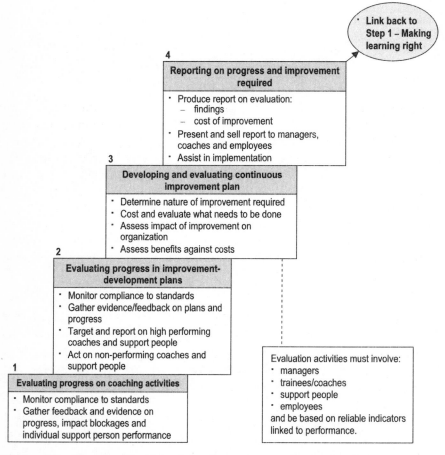

Figure 6.7 Step 5 – Checking learning success – the evaluation

This people management approach is designed to be a way of life. People management is an expensive investment that requires constant surveillance of activities and evidence-gathering on the extent to which the outcomes sought have been achieved, and on the extent to which all the activities and standards have been complied with. It does not mean focusing on just learning and training. It involves all activities.

It requires the same approach as specified in the rigour set by international quality standards. There must be evidence of compliance and action to renew. The evaluation must involve:

- managers;
- trainees/coaches;
- trainers;
- support personnel;
- employees.

One of the key questions is, who should conduct the evaluation? We argue that it should be those who have introduced the people management approach, set it up and trained the line managers to be coaches. Whilst the on the job learning application may have been handed to internal support people, it is imperative to ensure that non-biased collection of evidence and hard hitting, honest feedback is provided. The financial investment by the organization ought to demand it.

This is not a chapter about evaluation as such. It is about obtaining evidence on the extent to which the organization's investment is having the desired impact. This means evidence of:

- coaches operating effectively inside and outside the workplace;
- effectiveness relating to the detection of underperformance in areas of competence and behaviour;
- stewarding (whatever name you choose), if used, providing the level of support required and that this support is having a real impact on the work of coaches;
- improvement plans being developed; that they are meeting individual and team learning needs and having a direct impact on improving the way work is done and employees are behaving to the code of conduct whilst doing their work;
- the cost of improvement being related to real monetary gains in the workplace, for example:
  - improved safety performance,
  - reduction in rework,
  - improved equipment reliability,

- reduction in absenteeism,
- reduction in customer returns,
- improved team/workplace morale,
- reduction in customer complaints.

These are only some of the indicators listed in sub-steps 1 to 4 of the evaluation. The important thing is that these should not become too cumbersome in number and are able to be monitored progressively during the entire introduction and operation of the people management approach.

Evaluation is not a one-off activity. Activities that make up evaluation should be informal and formal. Non-compliance must be targeted immediately and dealt with as it occurs. The formal evaluation should provide the evidence, activities and suggestions for continuous improvement. These are fed back into Step 1. Making learning right – the structure. So the process begins again with total confidence that the people management approach is working and getting better (continuously improving).

SUMMARY

Developing coaches for managing people is a considerable challenge. Be prepared for some surprises if you are involved in the process. You will find that a number of line managers may not be able to cope. It will ultimately become clear they were not the right people for the job anyway. Others will find the learning/training a challenge. This should be viewed as encouraging. Learning ought to be a challenge; it should be difficult in parts but it should also be enjoyable. To succeed at learning is a great step to further growth. 'The sweet smell of success' does wonders for ongoing development.

The learning process will change all those involved. Each participant will become more confident. Each will think more about the employees who work for them. Greater thought will be given to how to handle/manage team members; more important, how to get the best out of each and, in particular, how to develop each employee further by providing the competence and confidence required to perform, behave and enjoy work.

Those who are unable to cope will respond in a variety of ways. Some may leave, others will require discipline. Ultimately those under discipline may become the target for dismissal. These people will join those, if any, on the team who have reached a point when dismissal is the only solution. The next chapter takes up this critical process.

NOTES

1. Our experience is that just because some employees are known to be difficult on the job, it will not necessarily flow over to their behaviour during a formal review. On the contrary, if the people management system has been well sold, many of these 'difficult' employees respond with support and enthusiasm.

2. This model was suggested by Ian Gribble of the Office of Training and Further Education, Victoria, who called it a 'Training Transfer Model' involving the trainer, trainees and management.

7

The road to goodbye: when dismissal is the only solution

BACKGROUND

In all of the previous chapters we have emphasized a coaching approach (and all that entails) for dealing with underperformance and/or poor conduct, with a confident expectation that coaching would fix the problem. Unfortunately, this will not always be the case and you will be forced to move from the coaching mode to your organization's disciplinary procedures, because it would clearly be inappropriate for you to allow things to continue as they are.

Reality strikes

You wake up one morning (or perhaps in the middle of the night) and you realize it is not going to work! Not your car (or your marriage), but a workplace relationship with a team member. You have tried everything but it now seems inevitable – the person has to go in the best interests of the organization (and the quicker the better).

The problem is, you have played this out as though it were always going to be OK. You selected the team member, you inducted and trained the person – you have been the coach. The person seemed pleasant enough and picked up the skills quite quickly by comparison with others you have recruited. So much so that when their three month probation was coming up and HR asked you to consider whether to offer a permanent position, you hardly gave it a thought. The person seemed fine.

Now we are 18 months down the line and you spend an hour every day trying to manage this person. Mistakes are made and the quality of work is poor. The person doesn't seem to care, comes late, absenteeism has increased and his or her attitude to you and other team members is extraordinarily negative. Everyone wants this person gone, including your boss, and you are not sure what to do or how.

You are not alone! There would be few people reading this book who haven't had the experience and believe us, if you haven't (and you continue to be involved in managing people) you will, because people are human – they change. Things happen at home that impact on the workplace. Not everyone can get promoted, people perceive jealousy and favouritism, and people get 'cliquey' and exclude other people.

Workplace relationships will drive workplace behaviour and performance. If the relationships become strained, performance can fall off or behaviour becomes anti-social – or both.

So far we have talked about coaching – encouraging and recognizing excellent performance/behaviour, and reacting to underperformance and/or unacceptable conduct as close to the event as possible, to help get the employee back on the rails. Now we need to talk about what we do when this is having no impact and poor performance (or behaviour) continues. The coaching is not working. You will note here a subtle change in language. In the coaching mode we talked about underperformance – as we move to the discipline process, we are now dealing with poor (clearly unacceptable) performance. We will talk about one-off incidents of serious misconduct later in this chapter. For the moment we are talking about an employee who, over a period, has not responded to coaching interventions to rectify the problem.

CONDUCT AND CAPACITY TO PERFORM

We need to distinguish quite clearly between cases involving unacceptable conduct/behaviour and those involving an individual's capacity to perform the job to the standard required. Virtually all English-speaking countries (and a large number of others) have embraced the International Labour Organization's Conventions (Termination of Employment, 1982) in respect of employment relationships and dealing with workplace problems. This means that, although the words may be different, the underlying principles are the same.

Before we look at processes, it needs to be said that while concepts of 'due process' and 'natural justice' are common to all, the actual legislative processing will vary between jurisdictions. We do not propose to directly refer to specific legislature. You will need to take advice on these matters from appropriate specialists, either within or outside your organization. Even if you do everything we suggest, you may still be subject to unfair dismissal claims and they could still be successful. However, the processes we recommend will mitigate against the chances of this occurring.

Your organization should have a documented procedure for dealing with misconduct and poor performance. If you do have such procedures, you need to make sure they meet the necessary requirements of 'due process' and 'natural justice' and you must then follow these procedures to the letter. Whilst there is a legal reason for this, the common sense reason is just as compelling – everyone knows and understands what to expect.

Underperformance

The selection process should be able to ensure that a person either has the demonstrated capacity to do the job in question or has the necessary potential to learn the job in a reasonable period of time and then perform it consistently to the standard required. If the person comes to you claiming to be able to do the job as advertised, the probation period must be designed to ensure that this is the case. One of the most common problems we come across with poor performers is that their application interview and referee reports say quite clearly this person can do the job from day one. We then accept errors as being due to 'He's new' or, 'She has to get used to our system', and the person blunders on through the probation period. The fact is, people do misrepresent themselves at selection interviews, as we have discussed in Chapter 3.

Assess them during the interview/selection process. Wherever possible, have them demonstrate how they would do the job; watch them do it. As we will say a little later in our discussion on poor performance, expose them to the team members they will be working with as part of the recruitment process. Let them get a feel for what the person is like. It is not just the domain of the boss to do all the recruiting.

We have dealt with this under recruiting the right team (see Chapter 3), but we can't labour this point too much. Design the probation period to determine whether they can do the job to the standard required. If that means making it longer – make it longer. Assuming the probation period has been completed, you would expect that the person can now do the job competently, that is, to the standard required on a consistent basis.

When that performance slips, you the coach must provide feedback and develop a plan to bring about the necessary improvement. It is not enough to tell them to improve. The old 'You better pull your socks up or you will be looking for another job' is now past its use-by date. The employer is bound to do everything reasonable to try and get the employee's work up to standard. If our coaching efforts are not having the necessary impact, there is a point at which we move to counselling – the first step in the formal disciplinary process.

Four things are important here:

1. The employee needs to know that the approach has now changed and that this is a first step in a four-step process – a warning. Get your work up to standard and keep it there or, if the poor performance continues, a further two warnings. If they don't bring about the required improvement – termination of employment. Ensure that, as an outcome of this first formal interview, all of the coaching assistance (interventions) that has taken place is documented for the record.

2. The employee needs to know that help will continue – active training and continued individual development will be provided, but it is up to them then to deliver. They need to understand the impact of their performance on the organization's well-being, and that we cannot responsibly allow the poor performance to continue. They should be directly asked if there is any reason/explanation for their poor performance and/or any mitigating circumstances, and their response should be carefully recorded.

3. The best way to do this is with another manager in the room; the employee should be asked if they wish to have someone with them. For the third and final warning we usually insist, and if they refuse to nominate anyone, get a respected fellow team member to attend.

4. Counselling interviews need to be documented and the first one needs to incorporate (for the record) all the previous coaching and informal discussions that have taken place up to that point, including any incidents where coaching has produced improved performance/conduct.

It will always be your judgement as to whether the process is working, how long an employee should be given to improve, and over what period the warnings might be spread and still justify termination.

Conduct

If ongoing poor performance (incapacity to perform) is difficult to deal with, misconduct is even more so. Oddly enough, serious misconduct, that is, misconduct that warrants summary dismissal (immediate dismissal without notice) is often easier to deal with than ongoing misconduct, which can be extremely disruptive and frustrating. Summary dismissal does, however, always raise the question, 'Does the punishment fit the crime?'

A QUESTION

What would you do with an employee working in a food factory who, for a joke, fills up a food product with hot chilli powder and packs it ready to go out to some poor unsuspecting customer? What would you do to his colleagues who encouraged him to do it? Does this conduct warrant instant dismissal for one? For all? Fortunately the organization had a provision for suspension in its employment agreement and the company chose to suspend the perpetrator for one month and the accomplices for two weeks.

Is this what you would have done? The fact that none of them had been in trouble before, were good workers and were genuinely remorseful made the decision a little easier, but you can never be absolutely sure you are doing the right thing.

One thing is for certain: a serious application of the workplace coaching approach will help enormously in bringing these situations to a head, correcting the behaviour (and getting on with life) or delivering the ultimatum – 'Change your behaviour or your employment will be terminated.'

As with the performance area, the procedure we follow is critical if we are to have the particular behaviour/conduct turned around. Again, the four key principles are:

1. They must know this is no longer coaching:

    - this is a formal process with four steps (or perhaps less if the misconduct is bordering on serious – see below under 'Serious misconduct');
    - the second to last step will be a final warning followed by dismissal for a repeat breach for which there is no satisfactory explanation.

2. We will help them but they must also help themselves. They must be directly asked (and we would say encouraged) to provide any explanation, reason, or an event or circumstance that may have affected their behaviour and should be taken into account in judging the seriousness of their misconduct. They should be told to speak now if they have anything to say because a further wilful or deliberate act of misconduct could lead to the termination of their employment.

3. Ensure another supervisor/manager (preferably removed from the day-to-day management of the employee) is present and that the employee has a representative. If they refuse to nominate one, you select a colleague to be present.

4. All interviews should be recorded and the first one needs to incorporate (for the record) all of the previous coaching and informal discussions that should have taken place plus any particular training, induction or communications to employees about this type of behaviour.

As discussed earlier, the areas of conduct/behaviour for which clear expectations need to be established fall into two categories: a) those that are generic and would apply to every workplace, and b) those that are specific to a particular workplace.

Generic behavioural standards

These include (but are not limited to):

- attendance;
- punctuality;
- smoking;
- drugs and alcohol;
- sexual harassment;
- bullying;
- racial discrimination or abuse;
- honesty (with handling of company assets);
- OH&S;
- teamwork.

Specific behavioural standards

These include (but are not limited to):

- hygiene (food and health sectors);
- dress;
- appearance (hospitality industry);
- language/demeanour to customers/other team members/students;
- security;
- e-mail/internet use;
- examination severity/plagiarism.

The issue of personal harassment often arises as well. 'I've been treated differently to other people in the group' is a common complaint when people are pulled up for behaving outside the standards. This can be particularly serious for an organization as it can lead to claims against it. One of the most frequent problems with discipline these days is the stress claim.

CASE STUDY

A common case arises where an employee has been allowed to 'get away with' certain conduct over a protracted period of time. In coaching we have talked about early intervention – for disciplinary processes it is even more important. We are reminded of one such scenario: an employee with a misguided belief that he could effectively do as he wished in terms of coming and going in the workplace – leaving without permission, arriving late without explanation and then objecting strongly by walking away from his manager and refusing to talk.

The first time any of these things happened there should have been a formal one-on-one to explain that this was unacceptable and must not happen again. The next time should have been a written warning. Since there was no definitive disciplinary action, it occurred time and time again for 14 months. As it then gradually became formal disciplinary action, the employee went into a stressed state and perceived the manager's behaviour as bullying. The employee went on stress leave and never returned. The employee lost his job, the company lost money and a lot of stress was created for all concerned.

We say again that if workplace coaching had been in place, there would have been a quiet word as soon as any minor infringement was identified (or repeated). One cannot emphasize how important 'due process' is in these situations. As we said earlier, it is not just a legal issue, it is also a matter of perceived fairness – justice being seen to be done. Remember our first objective in all of these circumstances is to turn the person's performance (or behaviour) around. We have invested a lot of money recruiting, inducting and training the person and it would be a good result for both parties if we can get him or her back on track. But, if the person can't respond – he or she has to go (goodbye) and it is important that he or she is not reinstated because of a flawed process. We cannot therefore leave this subject without some discussion of the legal aspect of 'due process'.

The first rule is, if the coaching hasn't worked or the discipline process isn't working or you believe an employee is guilty of serious misconduct, then seek advice.

A failure to abide by the rules can be very expensive (legal fees and/or compensation) and lead to a serious undermining of morale in your workplace if the guilty party is reinstated. The courts have shown they will not overlook a blatant failure to provide natural justice. There is a New Zealand case where an employee was sacked for fighting (which resulted in a jail sentence) but received compensation because 'due process' was not followed. A better example worth recounting here is the case of *Shields* vs *Carlton and United Breweries (NSW) Pty Ltd CUB* (1999) (1) FCA 377 (8 April 1999). We are grateful for an excellent overview of this case put together by John Cooper and Adam Goodinch from Freehills for the Australian Company Secretary (July 1999) which we have summarized here.

The incidents that led to the termination of Shields' employment occurred at a company sales conference at a Queensland resort. The judge's description of Shields' behaviour is as follows:

> Mr Shields and another seconded employee behaved in a disgraceful fashion at this conference. There was a dinner on the Thursday night. It seems everybody in attendance at the dinner consumed considerable quantities of alcohol. Certainly, that was true of Mr Shields. He had multiple drinks before, during and after the dinner.

On the night in question, Mr Shields' behaviour included:

- abusing a disc jockey during the course of the night and, towards the end of the night, being involved in what Wilcox J (the judge) described as 'a very threatening scene';

- waking up a room-mate by lying on him or being present while his colleague did so;

- entering the swimming pool area, where other guests were present, either completely naked or naked from the waist down;

- ignoring the reproach of a senior officer and ignoring the instruction to put on some clothes;

- making noise outside the door of a hotel guest who was not part of the Guinness party, and exposing himself to her when she opened the door;

- wandering about the conference premises at 4.00 am with no clothes on in front of a female receptionist.

The judge said that, in effect, he appreciated the two employees were intoxicated but indicated his view that their conduct could not be 'regarded as acceptable in people whose job it was to promote the good image and reputation of Guinness Australia and indirectly, their employer CUB'.

There was evidence that Shields had been warned to behave himself at the event. Shields provided the defence which we alluded to earlier, in effect, 'Others have behaved this way and not been sacked, therefore I should not be sacked.' Shields ran a video of a previous conference (several years earlier) showing grossly improper behaviour for which no one was punished. CUB had a culture of accepting such behaviour and he said his employment should not be terminated. The appeal court decided that the events on the videotape were less serious, particularly as they did not impinge on outsiders.

The court concluded there had been a valid reason for the dismissal and turned to the procedural fairness issue. Basically you must give employees the opportunity to defend themselves and, as this court said, it must not be a case of going through the motions. The appeal court determined that Shields had not been afforded procedural fairness because of three main failures in the process:

1. Whilst it gave him an opportunity to answer the allegations of misconduct, it did not give him the opportunity 'to put forward any mitigating factors, for example a history of good behaviour or his successes as an employee'.

2. Shields was not given an express invitation to argue that dismissal was not the appropriate punishment.

3. Even if he had put forward mitigating factors, they would have been ignored because the managers conducting the investigation had instructions to fire Shields if the allegations were established. In other words, they were effectively told to disregard any mitigating factors or explanations.

The court said it is up to the employer to determine whether there are any mitigating factors and the employer must carefully consider these issues before deciding the action to be taken.

There have also been cases of employees being absent for 120 days in a year, being sacked, and winning their case because the employer failed to act earlier. More recently, a dismissal for being intoxicated at work failed with the employee being reinstated because the employer had allowed the employee to continue working even though it claimed he was intoxicated.

In essence, the sorts of situations described above may have been prevented, or at least had a different outcome, if a code of conduct and/or clear policies regarding behaviour had been in place. If they had then been acted upon (early intervention) the situations might have been nipped in the bud or at least been managed better in the long run. Clarity of expectations with instant intervention for a breach is the key to our approach.

In dealing with the counselling/disciplinary area, two other matters require discussion: serious misconduct, and dealing with complaints by employees against other employees.

Serious misconduct

The world of work has changed dramatically. Natural justice must be provided through the processes of the investigation and unless you can prove serious misconduct, summary dismissal (that is, without notice) is prohibited. Suffice to say here, that theft, fraud, assault, failure to carry out a lawful and reasonable instruction, and behaviour that is likely to harm the business or harm the health of another person, are all included.

Prevention is best. We mentioned earlier on the importance of establishing a relevant code of conduct/behaviour to ensure expectations are absolutely clear. The matter of intoxication is one that cannot be ignored. For all organizations (regardless of size) a clear written policy should be in place. Consistent with our workplace coaching approach, in larger organizations we support a policy that states that any employee who has a problem with alcohol or drugs should come forward and, if they do, we would use an employee assistance programme to help them overcome their problem.

In all organizations the policy should clearly state that people will not be allowed to work if intoxicated or smelling of alcohol. Where hazards exist in relation to equipment, vehicles or other potentially dangerous environments (for example, knives in abattoirs), a zero tolerance policy should apply and a clear statement that employees found in the possession of drugs or alcohol (except prescription drugs which should be notified to the employer) or found using drugs or alcohol, will be summarily dismissed or will be subject to disciplinary action up to and including termination of employment. With the latter of these statements, it provides some latitude for dealing with individual cases (if this is what you want).

Dealing with complaints from employees

Before summarizing this important area, here are a few words about dealing with complaints/grievances. Every organization should have a written policy which clearly explains to all employees that if they have a complaint or grievance regarding another employee (or manager) they should follow a predetermined procedure.

Again this is not just a legal issue. Yes, we do have a duty of care to provide a workplace that is harassment-free and, in particular, where behaviour of a bullying kind is specifically banned. But it is common sense that, if we want a quality workplace (which you need to develop for the workplace coaching approach to be successful), people must be given respect. The only way to ensure this happens is to set clear expectations (hopefully with employee input) about how people are required to behave towards each other. This includes a grievance procedure whereby an employee can confidently raise an issue and know it will be dealt with both professionally and fairly.

CASE STUDY

A classic case in this area is a large public sector organization that has very lengthy documented procedures for dealing with grievances but no real emphasis on early intervention/early warning signals or clear performance standards for managers. After a *year* of alleged bullying and harassment, an employee makes a complaint of over 30 alleged instances of bullying. An inquiry is set up, conducted by a senior counsel who then decides four incidents did actually occur. But because the complainant refuses to participate in the inquiry, the charges are eventually set aside one year later, meaning huge costs, a serious impact on people and their reputations, and a bad scene all round. Only because a new HR manager brought some sense to the process and introduced new grievance procedures, was the matter eventually resolved.

If a person wishes to proceed with the complaint/grievance after an initial verbal notification, it must be put in writing and submitted to the offender if you propose to take formal disciplinary action. In a team environment it is not uncommon for an employee to simply want something to stop. They don't want anyone punished, they don't want to make a formal complaint – they just want the behaviour to stop.

If you have this inappropriate behaviour dealt with in your code of conduct and/or induction programme, it is relatively simple to either go to the group (or the individual if you choose) and advise them:

▌ there has been a complaint;

▌ if it is accurate and based on substantiated evidence (and you have no reason to doubt this) it is a breach of the code of conduct (our expectations) and (if relevant) may be a breach of the law (sexual harassment, bullying or racial abuse);

▌ what the behaviour/conduct was;

▌ that no action will be taken this time other than this general warning;

▌ any further transgression will lead to disciplinary action up to and including dismissal.

If you have the workplace coaching processes in place, the majority of people will respond to this and the behaviour will be curbed. If you have no processes/procedures, code of conduct or anything else, you have a much more difficult task to try and change a behaviour which the instigator probably believes is quite OK. If he or she continues to offend, the organization may bear the brunt of it.

Conclusion

Four factors (at a minimum) must be taken into account to determine whether a dismissal was fair or not:

1. There must be a valid reason for the dismissal related to the conduct of the employee, or the incapacity of the employee to perform his or her job or operational requirements (redundancy).

2. The employee must have been notified.

3. The employee must be given an opportunity to respond to any reason given.

4. The employee must have been warned (in the case of unsatisfactory performance) or must have known that his or her conduct was unacceptable.

However, it is wise to have behavioural and performance standards documented and to ensure employees are promptly and clearly advised when they are not meeting those standards. Coach employees up to the standard you require and when you switch from coaching mode to discipline mode, do so definitively – employees must know that their future is now in their hands.

Taking stock

In Chapter 3 we stressed the importance of the coach being involved in getting the right people on their team. We have extended this role of involvement to discipline in this chapter. We have set the boundaries to assist in the role of managing discipline with serial offenders who cannot conform to standards of competence and behaviour.

Disciplining an employee is never easy, but it must be dealt with without fear or favour. We conclude with a reaffirmation of some key points:

▌ Know and abide by the rules that govern the management of poor performance or misconduct.

▌ Seek advice if unsure.

▌ The consequences for failing to do so might be costly.

8

A risk management approach to people management

Risk management, in simple terms, involves:

- *analysing* a situation/process or new development;

- *identifying* the risks that are present and the circumstances under which they could lead to harm;

- for each of the risks, *determining* the probability of occurrence and level of impact;

- *prioritizing* the risk situations;

- *developing* means to eliminate the risk or, if this is impractical, the means to minimize it and to reduce its impact.

These are the steps in the development of a risk management plan for any particular process or situation.

We hope that you have noted our references to risk management in earlier chapters, as the concept applies to managing people. Our approach to people management is a key tool, not only for continuous improvement in business performance but also in managing the multitude of risks associated with employing people in the business. Obviously it doesn't just happen by itself and in fact requires a high level of commitment from all participating parties within the organization.

ANALYSIS OF APPROACHES TO PEOPLE MANAGEMENT

Between us we have seen first hand perhaps 40–50 performance management systems introduced into organizations with which we have been associated; some as participating managers, but primarily as business consultants. As stated at the outset of this book, most of the systems we have observed have served some useful purpose but many have either 'missed the boat' totally, or started well and fallen to pieces over a number of years. Many of you (like us) will have bad memories of performance appraisal systems that took up an inordinate amount of time, effort and stress, and still somehow managed to cause more harm than good – this was our inspiration for writing this book!

Let's face it, performance feedback and coaching of employees are 'motherhood' statements – what can you say against them, in theory? People want clear expectations, they want to know how they are doing, particularly when they have done well, and even if they are not doing well, to be given the chance to improve.

If people management (incorporating regular performance feedback) is so sought after and so widely accepted for its value to the business and the individual, why then is it not put on a pedestal and universally present and successful in organizations? Simply because, in many instances, it hasn't been a high priority for managers. Until there are serious people management problems, or the company recruits a senior manager who understands the power of a successful people management system and pushes for its introduction, many (many!) organizations either believe it is not worth all the effort or do not comprehend the benefits such systems can deliver.

IDENTIFYING THE RISKS

At this point we intend reminding you of both the power of a *successful* people management system and the risks inherent in an *unsuccessful* system. These have been raised throughout the book and they are intended to reinforce some of our key messages/actions:

▌ More and more responsibility and accountability is being placed with managers at all levels of organized work to improve the performance and behaviour of all employees.

▌ Managers today operate in an extraordinarily complex environment. Managers do not have spare time – the emphasis is more and more on outputs and the outcomes.

▌ Most managers seem unaware of how changes to key result areas directly impact on the performance of their people. Agreed changes to what has to be done and how, mean changes to work expectations (continuous improvement). It is totally frustrating for people and confuses them when expectations are not crystal clear. Continuous improvement in systems, processes and people is an organization's way of life. Organizations that do not embrace continuous improvement will probably not survive.

▌ More rules, regulations, interruptions, distractions and e-mails continue to place pressure on performance and behaviour. Often these impositions create a level of pressure that prevents managers from seeing clearly how a people management approach will in the end save them time by having more competent and confident employees working for them and reducing the amount of time devoted to non-compliant behaviour.

▌ Employees more than ever seek feedback (positive and negative) on their performance and behaviour. They seek continuous development to assist them in being more successful at what they do.

▌ Employees want to be in charge of their careers and hence their lives, by being confident that, through their development, they are maintaining a competitive edge. Organizations that do not provide opportunities for continuous development are likely to lose some of their best employees to organizations that do. _A major risk is being unable to recruit and retain quality people._

▌ Unfair dismissal claims have rocketed in all of those countries that embrace the International Labour Organization Convention. Employers can no longer hire and fire at will – valid reasons are required.

▌ Risk management has become a mandatory way of life in all organizations. It is a way of doing business. There are no better examples than those found in hazardous industries, requiring a safety case regime culminating in the management of people and the consequences if this is not carried out according to specified protocols.

▌ A lack of risk management procedures and protocols have seen the downfall of major corporations and managers worldwide. This 'fall as you go' way of doing business has had an unfortunate impact on employees, shareholders and governments, in both economic and trust terms.

■ There are examples worldwide of occupational health and safety disasters resulting from inadequate risk management. A natural outcome of risk analysis is a strategy to eliminate or minimize the risk and/or its impact (prevention/mitigation). In many instances this should give rise to the development and implementation of performance standards and a code of conduct.

■ The failure of many organizations to set down performance standards and a code of conduct (expectations) more often than not leads to inconsistency in the way work is done. Inconsistent work practices open up the likelihood that risk management procedures and protocols will be breached, which in turn has the potential to be extremely costly, particularly in claims, death or injury.

■ Employee (people) management includes:

- clear expectations;
- early intervention;
- recognition and celebration of excellent performance;
- identification and planning to eliminate underperformance;
- action to continue the development of employees who contribute excellent performance.

Of course it is up to the individual organization to determine the probability of occurrence and the likely level of impact should its people management system fail. You will also need to prioritize these risks before moving to the next stage – developing the means to eliminate or minimize the risk.

Well you've now read most of the book – what do you think? This is a good news/bad news chapter. The good news is:

■ our approach works – you can seriously improve your people management (if you haven't already done so, you should read the case studies in the appendices. This book and its 'how to' contents reflect what we did in each of the organizations referred to.);

■ the approach we propose will deliver continuous improvement in the business's overall performance;

■ our approach can save the organization a lot of money;

■ our approach can also save you a lot of stress.

We outline some of the benefits of our approach in money terms and look at the cost of developing, implementing and maintaining a 'quality' people management system later in the chapter.

The bad news is that a people management system requires some things from the organization and the people within it. Time and money are the easy ones. Commitment, honesty, trust and ongoing support for your managers and team leaders are the hard ones. We now look at the linkages between our approach and the impact on organizational performance.

DEVELOPING TREATMENTS FOR IDENTIFIED RISKS (AN INSURANCE POLICY AND A DRIVER FOR CONTINUOUS IMPROVEMENT)

The process of setting expectations, ensuring early intervention (coaching), and regular feedback, is critical to the delivery of excellent results across key performance areas. We have tended to concentrate in our examples on the conduct/behavioural aspects. When we start to think about the costs and benefits of introducing our people management approach, we need to return to the key performance areas of the business.

Financial

We have to drive improved performance across the key areas of our business. For example, in some companies it may be reduction in waste in raw material usage, reduced spoilage or reduced rework. By measuring and managing performance through day-to-day coaching in these areas, we will improve the bottom line.

Occupational health and safety

You have probably heard managers say, 'You have to live OH&S at all times if the company is to deliver zero lost time incidents'. This is of course true. The question is, what does 'live' mean? To us it means setting the performance standards and code of conduct, and coaching to those standards on a day-to-day basis. These principles of course also apply to quality and service (in all organizations), as well as environment practices (eg, the forest industry), hygiene (eg, the food and health sectors), security (prisons) and most other performance criteria you care to mention.

Employee satisfaction/relationships

Are you an employer of choice? There is a school of thought that suggests that if the company is known for being great at looking after its employees, it will attract and retain the best. We are more interested in the ability to recruit and retain 'employees of choice', but obviously (we think) this is a two-way street. We want people who are reliable, prepared to work hard, fit in with a team, competent (or have the potential to develop competence), and are happy in their job.

Client/customer service

Does everyone have customers or clients?

One of the most difficult performance concepts to get across is that of internal customer service. This is based on a widely held view that whilst external customers/clients are critical to the business (without them you do not survive), internal customers count for less. These days this is a short-sighted, even misguided view. All elements of the business become critical to its short-term performance and long-term survival. If an internal customer relationship is faulty it will sooner or later impact on external customer relationships with a potentially catastrophic outcome – the loss of customers. Managers must look after the people who work for them.

Closed institutions

Perhaps the most challenging area for dealing with customer/client service is that of closed institutions. Institutions fall along a spectrum of closed to open, which loosely speaking might have mental hospitals and prisons as the most closed, and retail stores and restaurants as the most open. In between are some of the most interesting organizations in terms of this question of client/customer service – universities, schools and hospitals – where the customer is not always right because many do not see them as customers or clients. They are patients or students, and they are *considered* to be a captive audience. We ask the question – if sustainability is based on return customers, professional reputation and word of mouth, can these organizations afford *not* to treat their patients/students as customers? We say *no*.

Educational institutions are a good example. For far too long the customer used to come last. In terms of opening and closing times, standards of teaching, availability of support/assistance and listening to student needs, most adopted the equivalent of the early Ford attitude: you can have any colour car you want as long as it's black! The time is now for many of these organizations to grasp the nettle in terms of performance standards and code of conduct. The way the educational market is developing will lead to the implementation of quality people management systems in these organizations or they will not survive. People are now able to 'vote with their feet' and are doing so. Like elsewhere, there will need to be better selection, induction and development of staff with early intervention and regular feedback on performance. Better systems for reward (and punishment) need to be implemented, or the organization is in real trouble.

Without a people management system like the one described in this book, your people will not get there – and neither will the organization. People look for some degree of certainty and security. Clarity of expectations, ongoing coaching, early intervention and regular feedback (including praise, recognition and reward), help to deliver a more certain work environment.

THE COSTS

Well what does it cost to set up and run people management systems which are based on these workplace coaching concepts?

Design and development

The development of expectations in terms of both the code of conduct and performance standards will obviously depend upon the nature of the business and its size. For example, a micro retail business (less than 10 employees) could probably use this book as a guide and develop both a code of conduct and performance standards (largely customer service standards) without any external assistance at all. Provided it keeps it simple, the design of coaching and feedback systems (and the documentation to go with them) could also be done quite quickly and cheaply. It may need some help on the management of difficult employees, but the system will help make this more straightforward.

The need to adopt an 'insurance' approach

As with all businesses (but particularly the very small ones), these costs should be looked at as insurance costs. You give up your time (time = money) to do all this and then, if they work well, you wonder why you bothered. But believe us, if you happen to have a serious underperformance problem or a major breach of conduct standards, even a very basic people management system can save you a lot of money. (This is part of the risk management approach – how do we as an organization eliminate or minimize risk?)

Now consider the situation if you have to get rid of someone to protect the future of your business. One of the themes of this book is often everyone's worst nightmare – both for the person being sacked and the person doing the sacking. But the real nightmare is not being able to dismiss a person who has stopped contributing to the organization. Leaving such a person in place to continue performing and/or behaving below expectations can start an epidemic of poor performance/conduct, as others see the person 'getting away' with things. In our experience this lack of action will actually drive good employees away.

Unfair dismissal claims for most employees in Australia are capped at six months' pay based on an upper limit of about $90,000 in total benefits (around £50,000). People who could be entitled to more than this figure cannot access the Industrial Commission System,[1] but can take action through the civil courts where damages are theoretically unlimited. Reinstatement can, of course, be a real disaster. It is not just dismissal that can cost money. A successful claim for sexual harassment or bullying can be much more expensive and much more damaging to the business. Whilst many claims are settled out of court, awards in excess of $100,000 are not uncommon.

Ask this question: 'What's the cost/value of a disaster that doesn't happen?' In other words, how do we cost or value a series of actions or systems that are designed to *prevent* such an event from occurring? In the examples quoted above, an investment of, say, $100,000 is cheap if it averts even one successful harassment or unfair dismissal claim.

Whilst this is not the principal purpose of having excellent people management systems, it is an aspect of it we must give serious attention. Can you really afford not to have people management systems based on a risk management approach?

Our approach contributes a number of things to ensure that you maximize your protection against any claim that might be made against you regarding:

- negligence;

- sexual harassment;

- harassment/bullying;

- unfair dismissal; or

- victimization.

Let us briefly explain the contribution that our approach can provide. Negligence can relate to a broad range of activities that businesses undertake. Nothing can guarantee that an action will not be brought against an organization. If, however, another party does take action against you, or is considering action, it is worthwhile considering how the workplace coaching approach to people management can help you.

In simple terms, negligence means there is an action that you have taken (something you have done), or an omission (something you have failed to do), which you knew, or should have known, would, or was likely to, cause harm or injury to another person. This is not intended as a precise legal definition, but it is sufficient for our discussion.

The particular 'treatments' our approach provides

People management systems and the workplace coaching approach help prevent such actions and mitigate against any claim for negligence for four reasons:

1. They are based on a code of conduct (designed within the context of community and legal standards) and performance standards that are in turn linked to the organizational standards. They apply in respect to standard operating procedures, safe work practices, customer service standards, sound environmental processes, and overall quality assurance processes and standards.

2. The development and implementation of workplace coaching will never of course excuse you totally for some failure or incident, but the setting of clear expectations (standards) and the training and assessment provided as part of the implementation of the system, are strong evidence of duty of care responsibilities being met, and will themselves help reduce the risk of such incidents in the first place. In most jurisdictions, the test will be whether you have done everything practicable (and/or reasonable) to prevent an incident or system failure.

    In most workplaces this is not just a 'people thing', but covers a whole range of practices including machinery/equipment maintenance, safe workplaces and appropriate control systems. Whilst our workplace coaching approach only deals with the people side, history shows this is the major cause of system failure (human controls over engineering controls). In other words, excellent people management systems can reduce the risk of human error and, by definition, other system failures.

3. By providing for a coaching plan and intervention designed to deal with underperformance or a breach of the code of conduct, the workplace coaching approach will have people improving their performance quickly or changing their behaviour, or finding themselves in the

disciplinary stream and ultimately, if they fail to improve sufficiently, sacked!

4. The final aspect of people management based on a workplace coaching approach is the positive workplace culture it engenders. This should never be underestimated. Managers who have worked in places with a poor culture will understand exactly what we mean. One cannot put a value on a major change to the workplace culture; whether it is a better attitude towards the use of protective personal equipment (safety) or simply people working better together, the impact on productivity, service and performance can be immense.

Be careful – assess the risks!

In some organizations the concept of 'managing out' an employee has become code for harassment. This has led to a massive increase in claims from employees against supervisors/managers on the basis that they have been harassed to the point of suffering stress and then not being able to attend work, culminating in a worker's compensation claim (in Australia at least).

We cannot make the point strongly enough: if a person is underperforming to the extent that he or she is clearly not going to make it, coaching must move to discipline clearly and swiftly. The person must be in no doubt about the fact that he or she is not meeting expectations and this is now a disciplinary matter.

Half-hearted interventions when coaching has failed will not be good enough. The employee will rightfully say that he or she had no idea the matter was that serious. When you *do* make it serious, there should be no doubt about it.

The flipside of this are those managers who, having decided they don't want someone on their team, don't bother with the coaching phase – they literally 'go for the jugular'. People are isolated, not invited to functions or events, staff and resources are removed from them (if they are managers), they are provided with written warnings for trivial matters, and their work is criticized in an unconstructive way. Eventually the employee decides 'enough is enough' and resigns. The manager is now happy. He or she has achieved the objective: the person has gone. Success! Or is it?

It may have worked 20 years ago – it won't necessarily work today. If the employee takes professional advice, he or she may make a claim against the organization for 'constructive dismissal', that is, whilst the person may have resigned, he or she will effectively claim that there was no choice but to resign. In other words, the way they have been treated left them with no alternative to resignation.

Such claims are often difficult to prove but there have been enough successes for managers to be very careful about how they deal with poor performing (badly behaving) employees. We must first:

▌ set standards;

▌ coach;

▌ train and develop.

If this does not work, we must move to the disciplinary process quickly and deal with the situation decisively. There is really no choice.

In essence we have, over a long period, _analysed_ organizational behaviour, _identified_ the risks the organization faces in its dealings with its employees, _determined_ the probability of occurrence and likely impact on the business if something were to go wrong, assessed the _priorities_ and decided that organizations must have an effective performance management system _or they will fail_.

NOTE

1. They can achieve similar outcomes through either the Magistrates Court or through the State Supreme Courts, which set no cap on payouts.

9

Preparing your workplace

In short, don't! If you have never pondered this issue, you ought to now. In our book, *The Great Training Robbery – A guide to the purchase of quality training*, we spent a good deal of time discussing how an organization should develop a quality training culture. We did this through a market gardener analogy – preparing the ground (organization) for the planting of the seed in such a way as to ensure long-term success.

In the context of people management systems, we are now of the strong view that we cannot wait around until the conditions are perfect, that is, the ground has all the right nutrients, water and sunshine. If we do, the season and opportunity may well pass us by. Whilst there may well be some things missing, and therefore a risk, the risk associated with waiting too long is much greater. Just do it – you'll get better as you go, but make a start.

As with many other consultants, we have traditionally tried to ensure that various organizational change activities go through a preparation stage prior to the commencement of the main activity. Whether this activity is the introduction of performance-based training (learning), an improved assessment system, new selection or induction processes, or any other change in people management systems, the presence of a supportive culture would usually be seen as a prerequisite to success.

In terms of our approach (and particularly workplace coaching) we do not believe this to be the case. In fact we reduce the risk of failure by establishing integrity and credibility at the outset. This occurs because what we do is based on our workplace coaching approach to people management which, perhaps for the first time, is giving people a clear understanding of what is expected of them. The activities associated with setting up our approach provide the vehicle to both fix the problems within the organization, and begin to change those things that caused the problems in the first place.

We now think differently about preparation. We see preparation in the context of emergency surgery. It can't wait until all the conditions are perfect: it has to be done now. The objective is to fix the present problem and then provide an opportunity to put actions in place to eliminate or minimize those things that caused the present emergency.

BARRIERS TO IMPROVING PEOPLE MANAGEMENT

During the preparation of this book, considerable discussion took place about the impact that organizational culture (in simple terms, 'the way we do things around here') can have on the successful introduction of people management systems. For example, there have been numerous examples of organizations that have rejected the notion of people management, strongly resisted its implementation, or simply paid lip service to it until it was scrapped. We came to the understanding that, whilst culture was a potential barrier to success, if the systems were straightforward and simple they would actually help improve the culture through the implementation process.

Furthermore, we came to the belief that an understanding of organizational 'mood' – the organization's state of mind and the way it sees things – is vital and that changes of mood can easily work against the introduction of workplace coaching. In other words, organizations may have an underlying culture which is supportive but if the mood changes, the people management system could lose support. It is critical therefore that this is addressed during the planning stages to ensure ongoing support for the system at the most senior levels of the organization (sponsorship).

The third barrier we had experienced was the 'flavour of the month' or 'fashion' problem. Many readers will have worked in organizations where there was never any ownership of the people management systems by the line management. HR and senior management introduce the systems but the follow-through sustenance of the systems are left to line managers who have had no real role in the design or development of the systems. In these circumstances, any system, no matter how good, will be dead inside three years. So it is with our approach. Without real line manager involvement from the beginning, there will be no ownership. If there is no ownership, the system will not be sustained and improved over time: it will just fade away.

We accept that many of you will have had bad experiences with the latest, greatest fads in people management systems. This book has presented managing people as a common sense, simple process that should form part of every manager's day-to-day activities. In practice, workplace coaching is about as simple as it gets. Set clear expectations and tell your people regularly as close to the event as possible, that they have done well or that there is a problem that needs to be addressed.

As you can gather, we therefore no longer subscribe to waiting time. If we waited until the trust levels between employees and managers were high enough, or the line managers were all brilliant at what they did, we could wait a long time. The best approach to introducing these systems is just do it!

That doesn't mean the development and implementation of new systems do not have to be planned – of course they do, and planned meticulously. What it does mean is that working up the performance standards and code of conduct to establish clear expectations can start tomorrow.

GETTING STARTED

We need to start the introduction of new systems by bringing our people and managers together in an environment where actions speak louder than words. When you approach people to ask them how they believe we should treat each other and what conduct/behaviour should be expected as the standard, people are already starting to get the message we are serious. At this point you need to be confident and enthusiastic; if you're not, don't expect anyone else to be. You have to break through the façade and begin digging beneath the surface. This is where you will find the individual, group and organizational strengths and failings. This is what makes the implementation of new systems exciting.

In the early stages you expect managers to bring up issues like punctuality and attendance, whilst employees are more likely to raise issues like:

- workplace language;
- grievance processes;
- bullying/harassment;
- sexual harassment.

These are just a few of the behaviours that get brought up for inclusion in code of conduct discussions. The fact that we talk about punishment (and rewards), and document and circulate these codes before implementation, ensures that employees know we are not only serious but that they have a key role to play.

Similarly with performance standards. How can people be expected to know the level of their performance without clearly defined standards? Whether in a service environment (customer service standards), a manufacturing environment (OH&S and environmental standards), or food processing (hygiene standards), without the benchmarks being clearly established you not only won't be successful, you invite disputes over whether people are actually performing satisfactorily or not.

A critical aspect of our system is to clearly articulate expectations for both performance and conduct at a realistic level. Over time and through workplace coaching, we can strive for excellent performance by dealing with individual or team underperformance in a systematic way.

To achieve excellent performance all employees must relate to the concept of continuous improvement – the pursuit of individual best and team best. We stress again, no matter how poor the present culture may be or appear to be – make a start.

To get a total commitment to continuous improvement we require a work culture that has clearly defined work expectations (performance standards and code of conduct), and people who are ready, willing and able to engage in feedback that is timely, valid, reliable, fair and consistent. They will support it because it is performance-based, contains no surprises, and ensures excellent performance is celebrated, whilst underperformance is managed in a way that produces positive improvements in our people.

A good example of this is performance improvement plans. They provide significant development opportunities for our people. The approach to learning can stretch across a broad spectrum of activities:

- one-to-one coaching/mentoring;

- job rotations;

- secondments;

- project work;

- work placements and exchanges;

- work schemes;

- participation in consultative groups.

These activities will deliver improved and confident performance that is assessed and sustainable over time. Without these tight connections between learning and performance development, we argue the effort and expense will be wasted. We believe that, more often than not, the failure of individuals to comply with work safety and environmental standards is due to poor learning design.

The whole objective of employees working and learning together is that each individual takes responsibility for performing to expectations and for improving their own performance where necessary. Continuous improvement in performance must not be seen as something managers do to workers but something which involves all employees; a dual mandate where managers and workers do it together. The very nature of work is that it is inextricably linked to learning. We strive for a workplace where employees learn as they work and powerful learning is workplace learning! We work hard together to develop workplaces where eventually the workers teach themselves, so as to sustain continuous improvement in everything they do.

The process of managing performance and the pursuit of its continuous improvement should be seen as the lifeblood of organizational life.

A REMINDER OF THE NINE PRINCIPLES

A good place to finish is our nine principles of managing people, discussed in the Introduction to this book. We produced these as the nine steps and they are set out as building blocks in Figure 9.1. Read them again before moving on.

In reminding you of these, it is important to reinforce the point that sacking people comes at a high financial, emotional and personal cost to those involved, and while you will never prevent all dismissals, you can reduce the number of sacked people as a by-product of getting better performance and behaviour.

Of course these nine steps have to be managed and this is where our people management approach comes in. It is about managing people on a day-to-day basis and is designed to be particularly useful at the middle manager and operational levels.

To move through the nine steps you will need to be very clear about the key activities that drive people management. Our emphasis is on the development of a people management process that we believe is easy to comprehend, learn, put into practice and maintain.

You have now read the book, so you can make a judgement about how easy it is to comprehend and to learn. As far as putting it into practice and maintaining it is concerned, you will not know that until you have 'finished

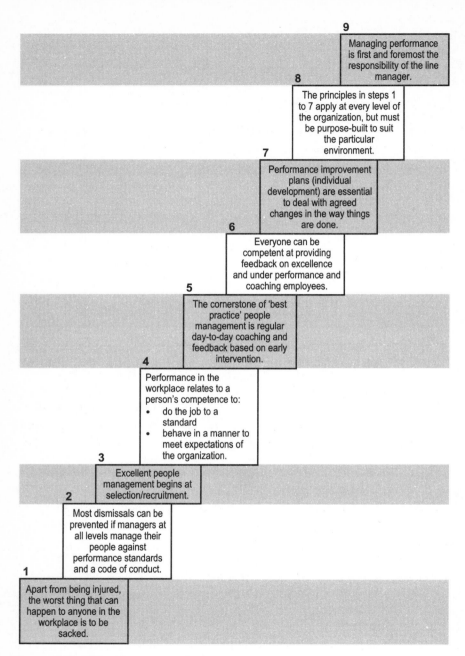

Figure 9.1 What we are on about

starting' and 'begun finishing'! The system is designed so that the managers in your organization can create a corridor through which all employees can find enjoyment and safety in what they do, and explore new ways of individual development/learning and adding meaning to their work.

The corridor will only become open through a common purpose and language that is based on management:

I providing leadership through commitment and role modelling;

I planning the people management system with all managers and team members;

I communicating the people management system, its principles and practice, to all those affected by it;

I coaching the work team;

I sticking to the plan.

It also relies on workers:

I making a commitment to work to standards of performance and a code of conduct;

I providing feedback to each other on excellent performance and underperformance;

I accepting responsibility for their individual day-to-day performance and continuous improvement/development where deemed necessary;

I taking responsibility to ensure work is enjoyable and everyone experiencing that enjoyment and safety;

I accepting that continuous improvement means lifelong learning/development – it does not end;

I delivering sustainable performance on a day-to-day basis.

For this to happen, everyone in the organization needs to see themselves as engaged in learning. This is not a new approach, but it is one that is valued and respected in the spirit of the cooperative endeavours it echoes in those organizations which achieve it. It is important that we strive to achieve this as it will continue to provide the way forward for all current and future employees.

THE LAST WORD

Sadly we conclude this book with some reflections on the recent headlines about chief executive officers and senior managers who have watched over the demise of a number of previously successful companies. We would argue that board members and senior management need a version of people management to set up expectations regarding behaviour and performance over the length of their employment, instead of year by year. This action may do something to prevent firms being destroyed, employees losing their jobs and shareholders losing money, while the manager who was responsible and supposedly accountable for these things, walks away with millions for their failed performance. We take up the issue of managing and rewarding the performance of senior managers in Appendix 4.

Happily though, we now know that these managers are being treated the way they ought to be – placed on trial and dealt with by the courts. We believe this is a turning point, a return to the good old days when business ethics were an unwritten way of life, but with the addition of continuous employee improvement being paramount for business survival.

Keep this in mind as you begin to put people management into practice and maintain it. In conclusion, we leave you with our best message: simplicity can be so moving!

Appendix 1:

Terminology

An understanding of the following words/phrases is fundamental to our concepts of managing people and your ability to understand and implement the contents of this book.

Capability An individual's overall competence, confidence and workplace behaviour.

Coaching Coaching is the continuous interaction and ongoing intervention to sustain and improve the performance of the individual and team. (Intervention for the purposes of coaching may occur at any time, but particularly when a coach detects excellent performance or underperformance.)

Code of conduct An agreed set of 'dos and don'ts' that govern workplace behaviour.

Competence The knowledge, skills and attitudes required to perform in a manner that meets predetermined performance criteria/standards. Skills incorporate the whole range of practical skills, low level thinking skills (conceptual and procedural), and high level thinking skills (trouble-shooting, diagnostic, problem solving). A person will therefore be deemed competent when he or she performs consistently to the specified standards. Competence is measured at the task level and is spelt out with great precision.

Culture (organization) Represents the way of life of people within the organization; simply stated, 'the way we do things around here'.

Excellence Sustained performance and behaviour above and beyond the minimum performance standards.

Expectations Simply, what the manager expects of employees in terms of performance standards and behaviour, and what employees expect in the terms and conditions of employment, the work environment, and the nature of the work itself.

Key result areas These are determined at the strategic level of the organization and are the responsibility of senior managers. They are translated into strategic objectives and flow down into a set of actions to be undertaken. These actions will ultimately affect employees on the shop floor whose performance is related to the key result area(s). It is critical their performance is linked to the process through the development of performance criteria against which they can be measured.

Line manager/supervisor/team leader Any person who has responsibility for the performance (results) and behaviour of any individual or group in the workplace.

Performance In a workplace sense, performance means the carrying out of activities to achieve a result.

Performance standards Criteria by which overall work performance can be judged; along with a code of conduct (behaviour), they are measures of actual work which require competence. They are developed from key result areas and need to be as few in number as possible to indicate that the results required of a particular work group or individual have been achieved.

Risk management A process whereby the objectives and activities of an organization are reviewed with a view to:

- identify risk;
- assess the probability of occurrence;
- determine the impact/consequences of the risk eventuating;
- develop strategies to remove the risk or minimize the chances of its occurrence;
- develop plans to be implemented in the event of the risk eventuating;
- train people in accordance with the risk mitigation strategy.

Team members People who work together in a group.

Appendix 2:

Case study in the production sector

1. The organization

Location	4 sites
Employees	80–100 per site
Structure	Run as a division of a large multinational
Timeframe	2001
General features	Dangerous, dirty work; significant problems on all sites in respect to:
	attendance
	punctuality
	teamwork (lack of)
	high level of conflict
	poor cooperation on OH&S matters
	poor housekeeping
	work attitudes poor (leaving work station without authority, laziness)
Economic base	1. Better than previous years due to considerable downsizing but still under threat. High labour cost

Union

2. If improvement does not continue, could close down
One union – very strong, 100 per cent membership on
all sites. Very antagonistic towards management

2. Background to performance management implementation

2.1 Whereas the company had downsized and reduced labour costs significantly, they were still not making money. Labour cost was a significant factor in this with record overtime being worked, mostly due to the level of absenteeism.

2.2 Because of the high wage rates and double-time overtime, employees could take days off even after they used up their sick leave, and then make the money back by working 'extra' when their colleague was away.

2.3 The senior management decided something needed to be done to address these issues. They decided that they would introduce a performance management model, implement it (after training) and then sack all those employees who did not shape up.

2.4 Their decision to seek some assistance with the training led to us becoming involved. It was during the design of that training that the company realized that their strategy, whilst a good one, had four problems:

   i   ensuring ownership of the managers and supervisors who had to implement it;

   ii moving straight from performance feedback sessions to dismissal would not wash in the industrial courts;

   iii they had no plan for ensuring consistency across one site (let alone across the four sites);

   iv continuity of the system into the future.

2.5 We all realized that the union would resist the system if it could be shown to be inconsistent and/or unfair from a process viewpoint, and that designing the process simply for exit purposes was not going to be enough to sustain the system.

3. Designing the approach

3.1 The company was quick to grasp the need for a coaching approach if 2.4 (i) and (ii) were to be dealt with effectively.

3.2 They agreed to the need to utilize the first part of the training with the managers to gain some input from them about what was needed to deliver a successful performance management/feedback system. They also agreed that the system would be driven more towards an on the job coaching approach which in turn would lead to formal off the job feedback sessions, rather than jumping straight into the formal sessions and meting out punishment.

3.3 They accepted a need to develop performance criteria with descriptions of both desirable and undesirable behaviour to assist with the consistency issue. We also implanted a Human Resources person into the process to provide consistency and give some guidance/advice where necessary, and we were available for one-to-one sessions with those managers who required some help.

3.4 Clarity of expectations, early intervention and regular feedback became the basis of the approach. Training was provided in interpersonal skills to assist negotiation/conflict management situations and managers developed a protocol for workplace intervention (GIDAY, as set out in Chapter 4).

4. Implementation

4.1 The company felt there was no time for consultation with employees in general. They consulted with the union about what was going to be done and why, and briefed employees as to what would occur and when, and the consequences that could flaw the process.

4.2 We went out of our way to spend some time with the union leaders who were tough to deal with; very conscious of looking after their members, and 'smart'. The message we sent was that this process was fair and appropriate in the circumstances. Employees would have an opportunity to change/improve (they would get better training and development) and the company could not afford 'not' to do it. Whilst the leadership never said so, the clear impression was that they watched carefully what went on and, provided people were treated fairly, they would not object. This is important as it mirrors our experience with

95 per cent of the employee representatives we deal with. (The other 5 per cent will be discussed in a separate book!)

4.3 This decision to 'no consult' at length was based on a belief that:

    i they could not afford to wait;

    ii the workplace consultation would deliver little that would change things – the good employees would support the process as a great idea and the non-performers would try and destroy it;

    iii the faster we moved after the training, the more likely it would get traction with the managers.

4.4 The 'roll-out' occurred over the next six to eight weeks and generally went smoothly. The unions took the company to the Industrial Commission (court) seeking to have the process put aside as it had not been agreed with the unions. The commission said it was quite within the prerogative of management to provide feedback to employees any time they wished. Provided that employees had a right of reply, such a process could be used as part of the disciplinary process where employees' conduct/behaviour was inconsistent with their contract of employment.

4.5 The process continued to be implemented over 2001/2 and still operates today.

5. Evaluation of results

5.1 To facilitate the evolution of the performance feedback and coaching system, we worked with the senior management group to identify the objectives of the project and how we would measure the extent of its success.

Immediate impact

5.2 A number of employees (8–10) who were given negative feedback about their performance and/or conduct, complained bitterly that it was not fair as no one had ever spoken to them about these alleged problems previously. The company could not now use these performance standards/criteria they were seeing for the first time to discipline them (or indeed sack them).

Note: The company had directly agreed to treat the first formal feedback session as a 'benchmark review' as we had suggested during the redesign stage. Obviously their message had not been received by some employees.

5.3 This reaction was seen as positive. In a roundabout way, they were accepting that the codes/standards could and would be used in the future to address underperformance and/or poor behaviour.

5.4 A small number of poor performing employees (6–7) sought early retirement on the basis that they were not prepared to work under this sort of scrutiny.

5.5 A few employees were eventually sacked and the decisions were held up in the commission.

5.6 A number of managers were found to be incapable of performance managing their crews and were moved on – some to different jobs, some out of the company.

Medium term

5.7 We made contact with the company at the time of preparing this case study and were advised that the process continues on, intact. It had, in their view, been extremely successful on three of the four sites and the unsuccessful site has now been closed down.

5.8 Changes in management and the failure to review/revise the programme had caused some drop-off in quality, but the system lives on and still works remarkably well.

6. The lessons

6.1 The system/approach should have been applied/introduced for the managers themselves first. They would have understood it a lot better and those that were not up to it or not committed could have been replaced before we started with the operators.

6.2 Support of the CEO by physical presence at training sessions and inclusion of the performance feedback programme in weekly/monthly reports were very powerful in mustering 'political' and 'resource' support for the project.

6.3 We developed a good working relationship with the management team.[1]

6.4 From our side, we changed a programme with a short-term performance management focus concentrating on underperformance and poor conduct, to a programme that has set the scene for the next five years plus, in terms of continuous improvement through continuous development of their people. They still achieved their short-term goals and 'managed out' some people who should have been removed years ago. But more importantly, they have set up a process to improve the performance of all of their people on an ongoing basis. They have said to us a number of times that it was our influence that changed the direction and the results of the company.

6.5 The other considerable impact from our side was the design and development of the training – turning it into a participative learning process from what could otherwise easily have been a 'stand and deliver' presentation of dos and don'ts. It is a point worth making that when you are dealing with employees who work hard for 8, 10, 12 hours per day (and we mean *hard*), who are consistently on the move and moving from task to task, the training/learning has to be highly participative or you will lose them.

6.6 More time should have been spent on spelling out the performance criteria to go with the standards. (In their environment they do not believe greater employee consultation would have helped at all.)

NOTE

1. All consultants get attacked from time to time in terms of value for money and the extent to which they add value to the organization (versus rehashing what is already known and presenting the most obvious solutions). This exercise was a great partnership story. The senior management team from the CEO downwards participated in the 'coaching' training programme. They added wonderful local colour to the 'fishbowls' and role-play cases that we had the managers/supervisors work through. The partnership concept went as far as including performance management in weekly reports and linking the programmes' activities to day-to-day reporting on results. As a consequence, we can see how we dramatically improved absenteeism, punctuality and safety performance (lost time incidents fell drastically over the next two years).

Appendix 3:

Case study in the service sector

1. The organization

Location	Single site, servicing over 200 entertainment outlets which are basically franchisees
Employees	40
Structure	Run as a division of a large tourism hospitality group
Timeframe	2002
General features	Office administrative work, plus an operations centre working 7 days, 24 hours, 365 days per year, to service the outlets plus an on-the-road group working with the outlets
	A number of performance problems existed in the business
	There was little or no performance feedback at the time we became involved
Economic base	Strong – financial performance excellent
Union	A few union members but not a big influence

2. Background to performance management implementation

2.1 The general manager knew our work from a previous business and had come to the conclusion that a similar system was needed to establish and maintain performance standards, which he considered to be below standard. There was also evidence of underperformance in relation to four individuals and some behavioural issues. It appeared there was some harassment of some of the female employees but it was not thought to be particularly serious; nonetheless it needed to be dealt with.

2.2 Being a relatively small organization, the consultant carried out the project working directly with the general manager. His senior management were supportive of what the general manager was wanting to do, but did not become involved.

3. Designing the approach

3.1 The enthusiasm and support that the general manager demonstrated to the employees and the other managers virtually ensured the programme would be a success.

3.2 However, as is often the case, two managers and two employees were not particularly fond of the idea that their performance was to be managed so closely – a natural reaction given the laziness of the previous management.

3.3 Nonetheless, the performance standards were developed in a relatively short space of time (many already existed) and the performance improvement programmes for the managers were driven directly from the business plan. These direct linkages helped to convince people that this system would work.

3.4 The development of the code of conduct was particularly fascinating and taught us a lot about the range of behaviours people find appropriate in the workplace. It was clear that a considerable number of the younger employees thought that their mode of behaviour was acceptable to everyone else on the work site. They soon found out they were wrong, as participants in the process spelt out conduct they considered inappropriate. There was also a lesson in not underestimating or ignoring reports of harassment. It became clear that one situation that the management considered needed to be fixed but wasn't particularly serious, could have become extremely serious.

3.5 The training as usual was participative and helped sell the key concepts that were being put forward to the managers and the employees:

   i. early intervention;

   ii. coaching to help people develop;

   iii. formal development activities.

It showed the importance of these elements being incorporated in the individual development plans for both managers and team members.

4. Implementation

4.1 Unlike the case study in Appendix 2, there was considerable consultation with the employees, with the general manager and the consultant jointly conducting the sessions. The value of these consultations became very obvious as the greater majority of people accepted the introduction of performance feedback and the coaching model as a real opportunity for them to improve their performance and, as stated by a number, improve their job satisfaction.

4.2 The other interesting response that came out of these consultative sessions has since become a feature of the early steps of implementation in a number of other organizations. The management and the consultant went to the sessions to hear what the team members had to say, respond to it, act on it, involve them and give them some ownership. It was known before we started that at least two people (and perhaps four) had commented about the proposal in a negative way and would resist it.

4.3 In fact they asked a series of questions at the consultative sessions that had a remarkable outcome. One asked what would happen if people did not comply with the code of conduct. The answer was that, depending on the seriousness of the breach they would either be informally coached or formally dealt with under the discipline procedure. It was explained to the person that, as the team members had put together the code (not management) and since new employees would be inducted into the code both by a formal process and workplace coaching, the second outcome theoretically should never occur. If everyone believes in it, accepts the need for it and complies with the outcome, there will be a harassment-free workplace. There was no response to this at the time.

4.4 The second employee then quizzed us on the performance side of the feedback. What would happen if people didn't meet the standards? The answer was almost identical to that provided to the person earlier on conduct. Again, there was no response at the time.

4.5 The following week both of these people resigned within two days of each other. The attitude of the other employees and the managers to this was, *the system is already starting to work.*

4.6 Following on from the implementation, two managers were given their 'benchmark review' and they didn't like it. Negotiations with these managers followed and they left the organization amicably. In the case study in Appendix 2, we had both resignations and dismissals (which stood up in the industrial courts). In this situation we had four people go and no litigation at all. Through the implementation of this approach, two other employees have also chosen to leave.

5. Evaluation of results

5.1 The general manager has been quite forthright in his views on this approach. He has always been a 'planner' and as a consequence he believes this approach, which is an extension of the business plan into the individual performance improvement plans of managers and employees, has delivered the outcomes he had sought.

5.2 Business results have reflected the continuous improvement built into the performance improvement plans, and the employees have expressed a concerted view that knowing what is expected of them and being able to regularly discuss how they are doing and how they can improve, has raised their job satisfaction enormously.

6. The lessons

6.1 As with the previous case study, the involvement, commitment and competence of the general manager helped considerably in introducing the concept. In this case it was also aided by the overall quality and enthusiasm of the employees to put a system in place. The lesson is: involve the people in the design and implementation as much as possible.

6.2 The fact that the introduction of this approach would lead to better quality training and greater developmental opportunities was a big selling point with the employees and delivered a rapid improvement in their overall competence and confidence.

Appendix 4:
Managing and rewarding the performance of senior managers[1]

INTRODUCTION

The principles described throughout this book are equally applicable to the senior management group. The application of those principles in designing and implementing workplace coaching is, however, significantly different.

To begin with, the manner in which a CEO is managed by the Board has a whole different set of dynamics to it. While we will discuss this role in respect to leadership behaviour, when we talk about the code of conduct (read ethics and governance), they are the driver of performance improvement programmes across the whole organization and, in a sense, the 'head coach' for the senior management team. They themselves (the CEOs) are not coached. They are quite rightly held accountable for the performance and behaviour of the organization in keeping with the strategic decisions and directions of the Board.

Whilst this is not a book about performance-based remuneration, it is impossible these days to talk about managing performance of senior managers without talking about the link to remuneration packaging. But first some words about the performance management system itself. We have preferred to call this a 'performance improvement programme' (rather than performance management per se) because of the emphasis at this level on self-management and the very high levels (at least theoretically) of accountability and responsibility.

SENIOR MANAGEMENT TEAM CODES OF CONDUCT

Many senior managers will have problems with the idea that they should be subject to a code of conduct. We don't care what you call it, but once again we would say the name of the game is clarity of expectations. We would argue that you have to have a statement of what the organization believes in, regarding:

- ethical behaviour;

- governance;

- behaviour in the workplace.

Senior managers should be brought into the organization with a crystal clear understanding of those three areas, as well as performance results, time-frames and the manner in which rewards and performance are to be linked. Organizations could save themselves a lot of time, money and frustration (particularly with shareholders) if they thought about some of these things prior to drawing up the contract of employment. This would ensure that if the Board were dissatisfied with the CEO, or the CEO with another senior manager, there is a basis to terminate the contract which is fair to both the manager and the shareholders. At the moment it is all one way. Managers can behave in an unethical manner, fail to deliver on results, behave abominably towards other managers and staff, and even engage in illegal behaviour, yet walk away with millions and, on occasions in Australia, hefty performance bonuses.

We are not suggesting that in this day and age you can recruit (poach) good quality managers into the organization and have them sign a contract stating that if the Board don't think they are performing they leave with nothing, or a couple of month's pay. Rather, we simply need to draw a few lines and set some standards that ensure that a manager who breaches a 'code' in any serious way, or fails to deliver totally, is not rewarded to the same extent as an executive who leaves an organization having fulfilled his or her part of the contract completely.

CODES OF BEHAVIOUR

It is important that the organization deals with this issue by ensuring that the ethical standards, governance requirements and general conduct/ behaviour are set out in a clear manner for all incoming executives. If we had a criticism of what we have seen in these areas, it is that they are less than definitive as a guide to what is acceptable or unacceptable. We would suggest that this can be achieved without a bureaucratic or 'political correctness gone mad' approach. A concise but meaningful statement on these areas is not impossible.

From a risk management perspective, it is absolutely essential that lines are drawn between:

- friendly relations and communication with competitors versus cartel (price fixing) behaviour;

- prudent destruction of sensitive business documents versus the shredding of everything and anything that might be used in a law suit;

- managing risks in a business-effective way versus exposing the company, its shareholders, the employees and the community to loss and/or injury of their financial or personal well-being.

We could go on for hours. We could put up a hundred case studies but we don't think we need to. The following points are made:

- As with any other 'relationship', clarity of expectations and early intervention are essential to building and maintaining a strong relationship and dealing with any conflicts immediately they arise.

- The inclusion (or reference to) a code of conduct/behaviour in executive contracts is essential to ensure that both parties agree what is expected.

- The ethical standards and governance policies should be a joint Board/ senior executive document, which is designed to encourage modelling of ethical decision making and governance 'best practice'.

- The code of conduct/behaviour in the workplace should be developed for the executive group and be quite specific where appropriate.

- Early intervention is just as important at this level (or more important) than at lower levels of the organization because, while the risk of breaches may be less, the impact can be destructive to an organization's reputation, even to the extent of its demise (Enron in the USA, HIH in Australia, Parmalat in Italy are some examples).

We now move to performance improvement plans for senior managers as the vehicle for performance feedback and the 'executive' coaching model.

PERFORMANCE IMPROVEMENT PLANS (PIPS)

Our approach to this area of performance management consists of a number of key steps. Some are common practice in most systems–some may be quite different:

1. Identify key performance areas (KPAs).

2. Develop a key performance objective for each area (KPO).

3. Determine key performance indicators for each of those areas (KPIs).

4. Determine the performance targets for each indicator (target).

These steps are common to most of the systems we have observed in our dealings with a wide range of organizations. The remainder of our approach is, as far as we are aware, quite different:

5. For each of the KPAs, determine the performance timeframe. This will generally fall out of the strategic plan. Don't assume every KPA is going to be treated as something that magically is achieved over one year.

   A good example here is the level of share prices as a target with rewards based on one year. It is possible that one can maximize the share price for one or two years by undertaking activities (or failing to undertake activities) that severely damage the company's long-term earnings and indeed long term-valuation.

6. Have each individual manager examine their key performance objectives and develop a series of actions (tactics) to move the organization towards the achievement of the objective.

7. Bring the senior management team together to share the tactical responses and build on them as a team and finalize the organization's business plan.

8. Have the senior managers individually prepare their draft performance improvement plan based on the business plan, but incorporating:

   - what is to be done;
   - when it is to be completed by;

- frequency of review;
- by whom it is to be undertaken.

On the final point, it could be the manager alone, the manager with other managers, or with subordinate managers, in which case these tactical actions will be replicated in the others' PIPs to ensure it is recorded as a joint activity.

Set out over the next few pages are extracts from some actual PIPs for the positions of Chief Financial Officer (CFO) and Human Resources Manager (HRM). Some of the 'tactics' have been removed as they are organization-specific and therefore 'business in confidence'. There are, however, enough to allow us to review the structure, layout and rationale behind our approach to performance feedback and executive coaching.

1. Key performance areas (KPAs)

Typically, financial performance overwhelms everything else. This is under-standable up to a point but remember what we said earlier – this is managing to improve performance over time and it requires a balance. We would say that six to eight key performance areas should be ample but must cover the spectrum of delivering outcomes regarding the people side (customers, shareholders, employees and community) and the compliance side (OH&S, environmental, financial, regulatory, etc) as well as a specific category deal-ing with growing the business.

In the example shown for the CFO, it can be seen that the key performance areas include risk management, compliance and funds management. For the HRM, occupational health and safety, and training and development are the two examples we will follow through the process.

2. Key performance objectives (KPOs)

These are like any other objectives. As we used to be told when we first started writing objectives, they must be measurable and they must be achievable. From the point of view of measurability, we have to be realistic in terms of the cost effect associated with measurement. We subscribe to the old maxim (Peter Drucker we think) 'What isn't measured, doesn't get managed' (or, 'If you can't measure it, you can't manage it'). For the most part this is true – we just have to ensure a balance between cost and the level of 'calibration' we seek.

Let us look at some of the key performance objectives included in the extracts from the point of view of measurability and achievability.

CFO

Risk management	Manage risk situations to achieve zero losses to the company at the least cost.
Compliance	Ensure compliance with all relevant government legislation/regulations (taxation, superannuation, etc).
Systems management	Ensure systems are developed and implemented in accordance with the strategic plan, to meet the needs of both internal and external stakeholders.

HRM

Occupational health and safety	Manage OHS to achieve zero lost time injury (LTI).
Training and development	Develop and deliver a training plan that continuously improves the skill profile of both new and existing employees.

3. Key performance indicators (KPIs)

Remember that these are *indicators,* that is, they need to be indicative of performance. The calibration will not always be that precise and the parties need to accept this. They also need to accept that the indicators are not as critical as the performance improvement plan itself, which, by its very nature, will have a more strategic, longer-term perspective than measurement for one year. Finally, KPIs are *after* the event; our model requires performance to be managed *during the event.* Intervention as close to the event as possible is still the message, but at this level it is possible (and advisable) to develop 'before the event' indicators – an early warning system. This is akin to people leaving the same part of their meal in a restaurant or not ordering a dish – you know something is wrong *before* the numbers ('bums on seats') fall.

Let us review the KPIs in our extracts and see how well they deliver the outcomes we seek.

CFO

Risk management	Incidents/near misses.
Compliance	Breaches reported.
Systems management	Implementation of performance improvement plan.

1. SYSTEMS MANAGEMENT	**KPI and Target:** Implementation of Performance Improvement Plan				
	Key Performance Objective: Ensure systems are developed and implemented in accordance with the strategic plan to meet the needs of both internal and external stakeholders.				
WHAT		**WHEN**	**BY WHOM**	**FREQUENCY OF REVIEW**	**COMPLETED**
5.1 Undertake review of current systems (including Survey of Users).				Monthly	
5.2 Seek input for systems improvement – identifying gaps.				Weekly	
5.3 Develop System Improvement Plan.				Monthly	
5.4 Submit for budget consideration FY2005/6.				Quarterly	

Figure A4.1   CFOs – systems management

HRM

Occupational health and safety   Lost time injury.
Training and development   Implementation of performance improvement plan.

4. Performance targets

As with the KPIs, the targets are important but not as important as the _analysis_ of the result. What did we do that made it move in the right direction? We need to know so we can do it again! In other words, sustainability and continuous improvement is the message, _not_ simply hitting a target.

The relevant targets in the extract are of two words: _quantitative_ (a numerical measure) and _project-based_ (the successful implementation of a particular 'tactic'). We don't need to go through all of them, but the zero breach (CFO, systems management; see Figure A4.1) and the zero LTI (HR, OH&S; see Figure A4.2) are examples of quantitative targets. Examples of project-based targets would be the systems review and improvement project that are set out as below.

5. Performance timeframe

This requires an analysis of the strategic objectives (three to five years), as well as the business plan, to come up with a realistic timeframe and to attach to the period under review those tactical and operational activities that have to be undertaken to achieve the overall objective.

1. OCCUPATIONAL HEALTH AND SAFETY	KPI and Target: Lost time injuries – zero				
	Key Performance Objective: Manage occupational health and safety to achieve zero lost time injury (LTI).				
WHAT		**WHEN**	**BY WHOM**	**FREQUENCY OF REVIEW**	**COMPLETED**
5.1 Line Manager training in occupational health and safety.				Monthly	
5.2 Coordinate OH&S Risk Analysis project.				Weekly	
5.3 Undertake management education programmes in relation to equal opportunities, sexual harassment and bullying in the workplace.				Quarterly	
5.4 Develop plans to achieve a discrimination-free and harassment-free workplace.				Monthly	

Figure A4.2   HR – OH&S

In the extracts we have provided above, the OH&S and systems improvement projects are excellent examples of 'tactics' designed to deliver short-term outcomes that are linked to a longer-term strategic outcome.

6–8. Developing the tactics, the plan and PIPs

This section deals with Steps 6 to 8, which are areas where organizations are going to do their own thing to a certain extent. In determining the best way to approach this in your organization, it will be necessary to have the business planning group work with the HR people to eliminate any duplication that might otherwise occur.

The starting point is the strategic plan. It is assumed that an organization has some sort of plan to cover the next three to five years or longer. It is also assumed that this will be the vehicle for the development of triennial, biennial and annual business plans. If these documents are of good quality (and kept up to date) they will speed up the development of the PIPs considerably.

One of the difficulties we have encountered is the expectation that HR or Finance will individually do all the work to set up the PIPs. It won't work; this has to be a team effort. A small group of senior managers who are well informed about the strategic direction of the organization will need to work together to produce the right results in terms of KPAs and generic objectives. Senior managers are best placed to then develop position-specific objectives, indicators and draft targets for discussion with their managers.

Many organizations do not share these details amongst the senior management group. We recommend it and indeed, find performance objectives that apply to more than one manager need to be carefully managed in terms of determining the roles and responsibilities – even more so where it is a project team that has responsibility for a particular tactic.

Once the senior management team have their PIPs in place, they can begin to apply the tactics to their departments and set up PIPs for their direct reports, establishing clear expectations of the contribution expected from them.

For example, if we were first to look at the CEO performance improvement plan we would see how their tactics/actions link with the next level of management. In the financial area, an expenditure-reduction programme would be included in the CEO's PIP as part of a Board-driven strategy, would then reappear in the CFO and finance manager's PIP.

Another example in the human resources area is OH&S and the completion of all risk analyses, which would then in turn appear in the PIPs of the HR manager, OH&S manager, operations manager and the floor supervisors. In other words, in this system we can see the linkages between the _tactical responses we have planned to achieve our strategic outcome_ and the operational performance outcomes needed to deliver these within the relevant timeframe.

THE EXECUTIVE COACHING MODEL

The main difference between the 'executive' coaching model and the coaching model described in the body of this book is that early intervention is only likely to be achieved by a greater level of planning and formalization of the reporting processes on the outcomes/progress of the individual manager's PIP. At this level of the organization the approach has to be quite different to that at the operational level but the principle remains the same. People may see the difference as being the physical and time separation between the CEO and the actions of their managers, but this is only part of the story.

Even at the operational level there is an expectation that team members will perform to standards and conduct themselves appropriately in the absence of the line manager/supervisor. With senior management groups, the fact is that the level of activity and diversity of projects they are involved in means that the PIP has to identify the _frequency of review_ (this is included in the draft extracts shown earlier in Figures A4.1 and A4.2). This greater level of structure doesn't cause problems as long as the frequency of the review is appropriate to the activity (that is, not all things need to be reviewed weekly or even monthly) and the reviews are 'exception' reviews – we will only spend time on those tactics with which there is a problem. The congratulations can still be there for those that are doing well, but we do not need to analyse all those things that are working well – there is time for that later.

INCENTIVES AND REWARDS FOR SENIOR MANAGERS AND THE EXECUTIVE TEAM

As we said at the start of this appendix, the issues associated with managing the performance of senior managers and Boards and the nature of incentives and rewards provided to these groups, requires a book of its own (which we have made a start on). However, this book would not be complete without some reference to the incentives and rewards provided to senior managers as part of their contract of employment. (We will not deal with Board remuneration in this appendix as it would be too lengthy and whilst related to the topic at hand, has some quite different elements to it on the governance side.)

Where do we start? We have golden handshakes, golden handcuffs, performance bonuses based on share price increases, market share, turnover and anything else you can think of; options that may be free or discounted and which can be taken up in a good year and sold off when the manager feels like it. Some people suggest that this is an appropriate motivator for a leader who is employed to maximize the long-term wealth of the shareholders.

I think where we start is to go back to 'square one'. What should senior management remuneration be about? What are the objectives that we should be trying to meet? Obviously an organization needs to pay what is necessary to recruit and retain quality managers. It is therefore a matter of negotiation to strike the right levels. We do not want to get into minutiae of the process of recruiting senior managers, but simply repeat that clarity of expectations is critical to a successful relationship, which means that the measurement, management and rewarding of performance need to be clearly articulated at the point of hire.

The other principles we would urge be embodied in the measurement, management and reward of senior managers are set out below:

- Key performance areas need to reflect a 'Balanced Score Card' approach and not rely on one or two annual financial measures to drive bonuses and/or options.

- Where quantitative measures are employed to reflect reward for growth/ increases, the lower parameter should also be stated, that is, the point at which we would expect a dismissal to occur or the events that would trigger a termination of the contract.

▌ Performance incentives must be structured within an appropriate timeframe.

▌ Termination of the contract must be written in ways to ensure that poor performers leave with no more than their payment for notice.

▌ Research should be undertaken with quality recruitment and remuneration experts to justify the base salary incentive arrangements and termination provisions in relation to market norms.

We will now provide a brief explanation of these points.

Balanced Score Card approach[2]

This is not new and is basically common sense. The old days of reporting just profit after tax, earnings per share and the dividend, are long gone – just look at any Annual Report these days. You would think that the left hand and the right hand of an organization were operating independently when you see some of the incentive plans. Increase market share! The more you increase it, the bigger the bonus. No need for balance, so we just cut prices, reduce margins, increase market share at a phenomenal rate and potentially go broke in the process! Suffice to say, the incentives must also reflect balance – not only what targets you need to hit, but how you go about it. It is not 'hit a single target and ignore the ramifications for other key performance areas'.

Include 'unacceptable' performance parameters

It is all about managing risk. So why shouldn't the senior managers understand the punishment as well as the reward? 'Increase market share but it needs to hold for x quarters and net earnings must not fall below y' is more appropriate in setting expectations than, 'Here is the target – go for it!'

Timeframe

We cannot tell you what this should be as it will depend on the circumstances. What we can say is that annual bonuses as the 'be all and end all' of incentive schemes are often totally inappropriate. If it was decided to have an 'at risk' component in the salary of a senior manager who was developing a mine over a three to five year period, and we decided to provide incentives for 'rapid completion', two major issues arise. First, we could pay out a lot of money for a mine that never operates profitably (for whatever reason). Secondly, we are saying to a manager effectively, just get this thing finished within budget as quickly as you can. If the senior manager's incentives are reflected downwards in the organization (as they often are) we are rewarding performance/outcomes that could lead, in the long term, to fundamental flaws in the operational capacity (not to mention OH&S and environmental considerations), which is the antithesis of what performance incentive schemes should be about.

In this mine construction example the incentive scheme should perhaps be graduated upwards over three to five years and impacted by other relevant performance criteria in terms of the construction phase and the operational start-up. Whatever the reward system, it must reflect the strategic, long-term outcomes we seek, not just 'this for this fixed period' as they so often do.

Termination provisions

This is really one for the lawyers. The point is that over the last 10 years shareholders, the community and even governments have expressed their dismay over the fact that senior executives can 'mess up' so badly that they are to have their employment terminated, and still leave with millions, often in the guise of performance bonuses. It shouldn't be too difficult to write a contract that provides for a manager who is dismissed for poor performance (or conduct) receiving nothing in excess of his or her basic entitlements.

Recruitment and negotiation of terms

We don't need to repeat ourselves. Enlist some external experts and have them produce solid evidence of market rates for remuneration (or do it yourself) and then design the 'at risk' component in accordance with these principles.

In conclusion, we hope this appendix gives some managers (and directors) something to think about. In some countries it is not beyond the realms of possibility that in future years corporate law may make it illegal to pay amounts in excess of basic entitlements to senior managers who are being dismissed for poor performance or whose company finds itself in financial difficulty. Something certainly needs to happen and we can help by ensuring that senior managers are themselves performance-managed with clear performance targets and clear expectations of their conduct, both in the corporate world at large and in their own organization.

NOTES

1. This will be the subject of a future book, tentatively entitled *Managing the Managers. Management incentives – stop rewarding the guilty.*

2. Originally developed in the early 1990s by Drs Robert Kaplan (Harvard Business School) and David Norton. They named this system the 'Balanced Score Card' as it provides a clear prescription as to what companies should measure in order to 'balance' the financial perspective.

Index

Further reading from Kogan Page

Coaching and Mentoring: Practical Methods to Improve Learning, Eric Parsloe, 2000

Coaching for Change: Practical Strategies for Transforming Performance, Kaye Thorne, 2004

The Coaching Handbook: An Action Kit for Trainers and Managers, Sara Thorpe, 2003

Coaching Made Easy: Step-by-step Techniques That Get Results, Mike Leibling, 2003

Facilitation Made Easy: Practical Tips to Improve Meetings and Workshops, 3rd edn, Esther Cameron, 2005

Mentoring in Action: A Practical Guide, 2nd edn, David Megginson, David Clutterbuck, Bob Garvey, Paul Stokes and Ruth Garrett-Harris, 2005

Performance Management: Key Strategies and Practical Guidelines, 3rd edn, Michael Armstrong, 2005

Practical Facilitation: A Toolkit of Techniques, Christine Frances Hogan, 2003

Tales for Coaching: Using Stories and Metaphors with Individuals and Small Groups, Margaret Parkin, 2001

Understanding Facilitation: Theory and Principle, Christine Frances Hogan, 2002

The above titles are available from all good bookshops or direct from the publishers. To obtain more information, please contact the publisher at the address below:

Kogan Page
120 Pentonville Road
London N1 9JN
Tel: 020 7278 0433
Fax: 020 7837 6348

www.kogan-page.co.uk

ALSO AVAILABLE
FROM KOGAN PAGE

0 7494 4293 X   Hardback   2005

Kogan Page is Europe's largest independent publisher of business books

For further information, and to order, visit our website

www.kogan-page.co.uk

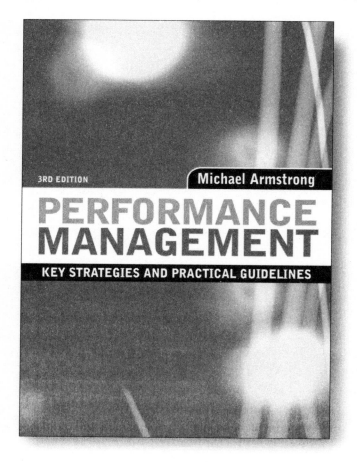

ALSO AVAILABLE FROM KOGAN PAGE

0 7494 4479 7   Paperback   2006

Kogan Page is Europe's largest independent publisher of business books

For further information, and to order, visit our website

www.kogan-page.co.uk